# Smoking and your Health

## ISSUES

## Volume 86

Editor

Craig Donnellan

**Independence**

Educational Publishers
Cambridge

First published by Independence
PO Box 295
Cambridge CB1 3XP
England

**British Library Cataloguing in Publication Data**
Smoking and your Health – (Issues Series)
I. Donnellan, Craig II. Series
362.2'96

ISBN 1 86168 287 5

**Printed in Great Britain**
MWL Print Group Ltd

**Typeset by**
Claire Boyd

**Cover**
The illustration on the front cover is by
Pumpkin House.

# CONTENTS

# Introduction

*Smoking and your Health* is the eighty-sixth volume in the **Issues** series. The aim of this series is to offer up-to-date information about important issues in our world.

*Smoking and your Health* looks at smoking trends and quitting smoking.

The information comes from a wide variety of sources and includes:
Government reports and statistics
Newspaper reports and features
Magazine articles and surveys
Website material
Literature from lobby groups
and charitable organisations.

It is hoped that, as you read about the many aspects of the issues explored in this book, you will critically evaluate the information presented. It is important that you decide whether you are being presented with facts or opinions. Does the writer give a biased or an unbiased report? If an opinion is being expressed, do you agree with the writer?

*Smoking and your Health* offers a useful starting-point for those who need convenient access to information about the many issues involved. However, it is only a starting-point. At the back of the book is a list of organisations which you may want to contact for further information.

\*\*\*\*\*

# Who smokes and how much?

## Information from Action on Smoking and Health (ASH)

### Number of adult smokers

The highest recorded level of smoking among men was 82% in 1948, when surveys started. Among women, smoking prevalence remained fairly constant between 1948 and 1970 and peaked at 45% in 1966. Overall prevalence among adults (aged 16 and over) fell steadily between the mid 1970s and early 1980s, faster among men than women, until there was effectively no difference between the sexes.[1] After 1982, the rate of decline slowed, with prevalence falling by only about one percentage point every two years until 1990, since when it has levelled out. However, an analysis of data taken from the government's monthly Omnibus survey demonstrated that between 1999 and 2002 there was a decline in adult smoking of around 0.4% per annum.[2]

There are about 12 million adult cigarette smokers in Great Britain and another 1.3 million who smoke pipes and/or cigars. There are about 9.6 million ex-smokers.[3]

**ash.**
action on smoking and health

### Cigarette smoking and age

Smoking prevalence is highest in the 20-24 age group for both men and women (37% and 38% respectively) but thereafter in older age groups there are progressively fewer smokers. Since 1996, young women in the 16-19 age group have been significantly more likely to smoke than men of the same age. Smoking continues to be lowest among people aged 60 and over. Although they are more likely than younger people to have ever been smokers, they are much more likely to have stopped smoking.

### Number of secondary school children who smoke

Very few pupils are smokers when they start secondary school: among 11-year-olds only 1% are regular smokers. The likelihood of smoking increases with age so that by age 15

22% of pupils are regular smokers. Overall, the prevalence of regular smoking among teenagers aged 11-15 has remained stable at between 9 and 11% since 1998. In 2003, 9% were regular smokers, a decrease from 10% in 2002. Since 1982, most of the reduction in prevalence has occurred among 14 and 15-year-old boys.[4]

### Cigarette smoking and socio-economic group

There is a strong link between cigarette smoking and socio-economic group. In 2002, 32% of men and 31% of women in routine and manual occupations smoked compared to 20% of men and 18% of women in non-manual occupations. There has been a slower decline in smoking among manual groups, so that smoking has become increasingly concentrated in this population. As in previous GHS surveys, the 2002 data revealed an association between socio-economic group and the age at which people started to smoke. Of those in the managerial and professional house-

holds, 30% had started smoking before they were 16, compared with 43% of those in routine and manual households.

## Tobacco consumption

Consumption of manufactured cigarettes among adult male smokers rose from 14 per day in 1949 to 19 per day in 1955, and remained at about this level until 1970 when there was an increase to 22 per day by 1973. Among female smokers, consumption rose steadily from 7 cigarettes per day in 1949 to a maximum of 17 per day in 1976. Since the mid 1970s cigarette consumption has fallen among both men and women. Although the prevalence of cigarette smoking changed little during the 1990s, the GHS has shown a continuing fall in the reported number of cigarettes smoked. The fall in consumption has occurred mainly among younger smokers, whilst the number of cigarettes smoked among those aged 50 and over has changed very little since the mid 1970s.

### First cigarette of the day

Addiction to nicotine can be measured in a number of ways. One method is to note how long after waking a person smokes their first cigarette of the day. In 2002, 15% of smokers had their first cigarette within 5 minutes of waking. Among smokers of 20 or more cigarettes a day, 31% smoked their first cigarette of the day within 5 minutes of waking.

*References*
Unless otherwise stated, the above information is taken from: *Living in Britain – Results from the 2002 General Household Survey*, Office for National Statistics, 2004. http://www.statistics.gov.uk/lib

1  Wald, N. and Nicolaides-Bouman, A. *UK Smoking Statistics*. 2nd edition Oxford University Press, 1991
2  Jarvis, M. Monitoring cigarette smoking prevalence in Britain in a timely fashion. *Addiction* 2003; 98: 1569-1574
3  General Household Survey 2002; mid-2002 population estimates: Great Britain, ONS, 2003
4  *Drug use, smoking and drinking among young people in England in 2003.* Department of Health, 2004. http://www.dh.gov.uk/assetRoot/04/07/96/61/04079661.pdf

■ The above information is from ASH's website: www.ash.org.uk

© ASH

# Smoking statistics

## Information from the British Heart Foundation

■ Every year in the UK around 114,000 smokers die as a result of smoking. This represents one-fifth of all UK deaths.

■ Most of these deaths are from one of the three main diseases associated with smoking: lung cancer, coronary heart disease and chronic obstructive lung disease.

■ Smoking kills over 30,000 people each year in the UK from cardiovascular disease. One in four smoking-related deaths in the UK is from cardiovascular disease.

■ In the UK, one-fifth of premature deaths from cardiovascular disease are caused by smoking.

■ On average, UK smokers who die in middle age lose 21 years of life.

■ About half of all regular smokers will eventually be killed by their habit.

■ Worldwide, smoking kills more people from cardiovascular disease than from cancer. Over a third of almost 5 million deaths attributable to smoking globally are due to cardiovascular disease.

■ In the UK today, around 13 million adults (28% of men and 26% of women) smoke cigarettes.

■ Around one in ten teenagers in the UK is a regular smoker. By age 15, more than one in five smokes regularly.

■ In both men and women, the proportion of adults who smoke is highest in those aged 20-24 years.

■ There is a strong association between cigarette smoking and socio-economic position. Around one-third of adults in manual households in the UK smoke compared to around one-fifth in non-manual households.

■ Rates of smoking are higher in Scotland than in England, Wales or Northern Ireland. Within England rates are generally higher in the North than in the Midlands or the South.

■ Smoking rates vary considerably between ethnic groups in the UK. In men, rates are particularly high in the Bangladeshi (42% current smokers) and Irish (39%) communities.

■ Smoking prevalence in the UK declined substantially in the 1970s and early 1980s and continued declining, at a lower rate, for another decade. In the last 10 years, however, smoking rates have remained relatively stable.

■ By international standards smoking rates in the UK are relatively low in men and relatively high in women.

■ In England, targets for smoking

rates in adults, children, pregnant women and manual groups have been set for 2005 and 2010. It is unclear if the target for adults will be met. The targets for children and pregnant women are likely to be met but the latest smoking figures indicate little progress towards the target for manual groups.

- Mounting evidence over the last two decades has shown that exposure to secondhand smoke, or passive smoking is harmful to adult and child health.

- Regular exposure to secondhand smoke increases the risk of both lung cancer and coronary heart disease by around 25%.

- Each year in the UK many deaths can be attributed to passive smoking. Estimates range from 1,000 to 15,000 deaths per year. The majority of these deaths will be from coronary heart disease.

- A significant proportion of the UK population are exposed regularly to secondhand smoke in the home – around 7.3 million adults and 5 million children.

- One in five non-smokers in the UK are exposed 'frequently or continuously' to secondhand smoke at work.

- Among British adults, while there is a high degree of overall awareness about the health risks of passive smoking, only two-thirds of adults, and less than 50% of heavy smokers, believe passive smoking increases the risk of coronary heart disease.

- A majority of British smokers say they modify their smoking behaviour in the company of children and non-smokers – 66% do not smoke and 21% smoke less in the company of children.

- There is considerable support among the British public for much greater restrictions on smoking in public places. Over 85% of adults agree smoking should be restricted in restaurants, work and other public places.

- Stopping smoking has a number of short- and long-term health benefits.

- Quitting smoking at any age reduces the chances of dying. The

greatest benefits are found the earlier the smoking cessation takes place.

- On stopping smoking there is a rapid, partial decline in the risk of coronary heart disease (about 50% decline in excess risk within 1 year of cessation), followed by a more gradual decline, with risks reaching those of never smokers after a number of years of abstinence.

- Stopping smoking soon after a heart attack reduces the risk of dying of a subsequent heart attack by around 25%.

- Stopping smoking before middle age avoids more than 90% of the risk of lung cancer attributable to tobacco.

- In the UK today, an estimated 11 million adults (27% of men and 21% of women) are ex-smokers.

- In Britain, the majority of current smokers (70%) would like to give up and over half have made a serious cessation attempt in the past five years.

- Numbers using NHS smoking cessation services in England have increased from 15,000 in 1999/2000 to 235,000 in 2002/03.

- Of those using NHS smoking cessation services in England, over three-quarters are prescribed Nicotine Replacement Therapy and over half report having successfully quit at their 4-week follow-up. No data on long-term quit rates are available.

- The number of successful quitters per 100,000 population using smoking cessation services is over twice as high in Health Action Zones than in non-Health Action Zone areas.

- Targets for the use of smoking cessation services in England for 2001/02 and 2002/03 have been met. Targets for 2004/05 – 2005/06 are more ambitious and a considerable increase in use of the service will be needed for these to be met.

- The above information is from *Smoking statistics 2004* published by the British Heart Foundation. For more information see their address details on page 41.

© *British Heart Foundation*

## Smoking and age

**Smoking prevalence is highest in the 20-24 age group for both men and women but thereafter in older age groups there are progressively fewer smokers. Since 1996, young women in the 16-19 age group have been significantly more likely to smoke than men of the same age.**

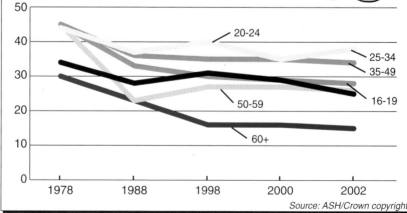

*Source: ASH/Crown copyright*

# Anatomy of a cigarette

## Information from www.TheSite.org

There's more to a tab than shredded tobacco. When someone sparks up, the smoke contains almost 4,000 chemicals, many of which are harmful to health. TheSite takes a deep breath, and asks, what's inside a cigarette?

Of all the stuff crammed into a smoke, the three biggest harmful components are nicotine, carbon monoxide and tar.

### Nicotine

The damage to health may be caused by the tar and poisonous chemicals, but it's the nicotine in tobacco which smokers can grow to depend upon.

Nicotine is a powerful and fast-acting stimulant drug. In small doses, it speeds up heart rate and increases blood pressure. This makes smokers feel more alert when they light up, while the brain activates a 'reward' system which is thought to be responsible for the pleasurable, relaxing 'hit' they describe.

The effect on an individual smoker depends on a number of different factors:

- Physical build and current state of health
- The length of time they have been smoking
- How frequently they smoke
- The number of puffs they take, and how deeply the smoke is inhaled.

### Tar

Ciggie smoke condenses when it's inhaled. This is a bit like watching droplets form upon the ceiling above a boiling kettle. The end result with smoking, however, is a whole lot more black and sticky. In fact about 70% of the tar present in tobacco smoke gets dumped into the lungs. It contains many substances which have been linked with cancer, as well as irritants that cause the narrow airways inside the lungs to get inflamed and clogged with mucus.

### Carbon monoxide

This is a poisonous gas found in high concentration in cigarette smoke, not to mention the stuff which coughs out of car exhaust pipes. Once inside the lungs, the carbon atoms grab any passing haemoglobin (the oxygen-forming substance found in the blood) and basically take a joy ride around the body.

Someone who smokes 20 a day can have a carbon monoxide level which is 5-10 times that of a non-smoker. This deprives the body of oxygen, which makes the blood sticky and can cause problems with the growth, repair and exchange of healthy nutrients. In particular, any reduction in oxygen levels is a real hazard to unborn babies. Pregnant women who smoke run a serious risk of miscarrying or having babies with low birth rate.

Ultimately, carbon monoxide can mess up electrical activity in the heart and encourage fatty deposits to clog up artery walls.

### Bizarre chemicals present in tobacco smoke:

- Formaldehyde: used for pickling things in jars.
- Acetone: found in nail varnish.
- Ammonia: used in fertiliser.
- Hydrogen sulphide: smells of rotten eggs.
- Polonium: a radioactive component
- Arsenic: a killer poison

■ QUIT Helpline for smokers who want to stop and people trying to remain as ex-smokers can be contacted at stopsmoking@quit.org.uk or call Quitline on 0800 002200.

■ The above information is from www.TheSite.org TheSite.org aims to offer the best guide to life for young adults, aged 16-25.

*© www.TheSite.org*

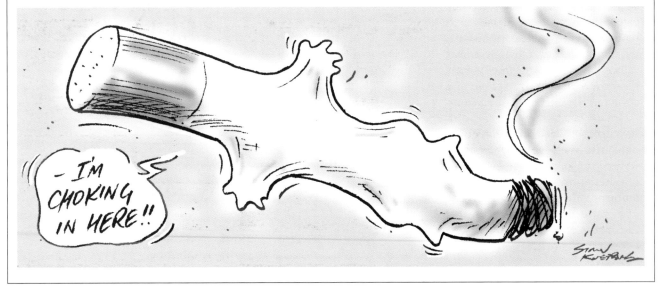

# Real drag

## Teenage smoking in the UK

Eighty per cent of UK smokers start as teenagers. Our teenage smoking rates are amongst the highest in Europe, and, at 15 and 16, the highest. A fifth of young people start smoking before the age of 14. By 11, one-third, and by 16, two thirds, have experimented with cigarettes.

Teenage smoking is something which, like bad hair or bad music, many adults associate with teenage rebellion. It's obnoxious, inappropriate and unattractive, they reason, but it's often a mistake, a phase. Something unsettling but ultimately harmless.

Two reasons not to be complacent. One, teenage smokers do not find it easy to quit. The majority smoke well into adulthood. Two, teenage smoking causes permanent genetic damage, which raises the risk of lung (and, for girls, breast) cancer significantly, whether or not the smoker later stops.

Hollywood is often blamed for the prevalence of teen smoking. Today's films are the smokiest since 1950. Studies have indicated that teenage film fans are more likely to smoke if their favourite stars light up on screen. The fact that many celebrities smoke, off screen if not on, is common knowledge, broadcast loud by tabloid exposés.

TV shows like *No Angels*, and 'reality television' shows, which often cater to a massive teen audience, feature near-constant smoking. Certainly, the UK's biggest reality shows, *I'm a Celebrity, Get Me Out of Here!* and *Big Brother*, promote a distorted view of smoking frequency.

The glamorous, and healthy, image of many smoking stars contradicts the message that smoking wrecks your looks and threatens your life. Models are perceived, at least, as amongst the heaviest smokers. Photos of Kate Moss, Naomi Campbell and Gisele Bundchen dangling cigarettes are priceless tobacco ads.

### QUIT
Helping smokers to quit

Part of the problem is that apparently condemnatory stories on celebrity smoking habits spread alluring photos across the press. A feature on a soap starlet 'sneaking out for a sly ciggie' at an award ceremony, and the accompanying photo or sequence of photos, cannot but glamorise the habit in the eyes of a certain audience.

For most of the twentieth century, men smoked considerably more heavily than women. The gap has narrowed fast in recent decades. Now 28% of UK men, and 26% of UK women, smoke. Teenage girls, though, smoke more, a lot more, than teenage boys: 26%:21% at 15.

Until awareness of the health threat was near universal, the cigarette was the advertiser's dream: the ultimate blank canvas product. Smoking could be sold as macho, raw, military, or as refined, elegant, sophisticated. James Bond smoked, so did Vietnam heroes. So did Marlene Dietrich and Audrey Hepburn.

The emergence of solid smoking fact has undermined the macho image of smoking more completely than it has the feminine. The idea of action heroes taking a fag break doesn't wash. But the City girl having a smoke: why not? It's ironic that nicotine dependence should've been seen for decades as a sign of independence in women. The label lingers, though, and female smokers remain more likely to be portrayed as feisty, tough, in control. They're also more likely, thanks to tobacco's appetite suppressant properties, to be seen as thin. The 'sassy' and 'skinny' tags lend the noxious habit an immense allure.

Image is often seen as a major force behind teenage smoking. It taps into celebrity and into notions of rebellion, control and independence. Peer pressure pushes the image agenda by promoting the alienation of 'sad' non-smokers.

The main reason teenagers give for smoking, though, is not image or peer pressure, not addiction or enjoyment, but stress. Cigarettes are still seen, by teenagers and by the adult population, as a relaxant. To what extent the stress cited is real, and to what extent part of an aspiration to a busy 'adult' lifestyle, so actually an image factor, hasn't been determined.

The fact that smoking prevalence is highest overall in the 20-

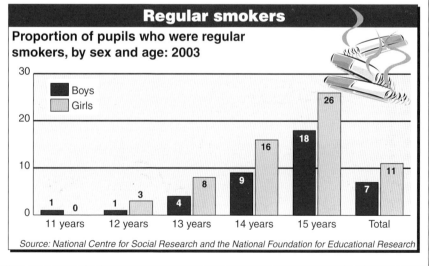

**Regular smokers**

Proportion of pupils who were regular smokers, by sex and age: 2003

- Boys
- Girls

| | 11 years | 12 years | 13 years | 14 years | 15 years | Total |
|---|---|---|---|---|---|---|
| Boys | 1 | 1 | 4 | 9 | 18 | 7 |
| Girls | 0 | 3 | 8 | 16 | 26 | 11 |

*Source: National Centre for Social Research and the National Foundation for Educational Research*

24 age group backs up a theory that many young people are taking up the habit with the intention of smoking for a few years, then giving up, and that a proportion are stopping in their twenties or thirties. They see radiant celebrities enjoying a few nicotine-fuelled years before quitting very publicly and don't see why they shouldn't do the same.

Why shouldn't they do the same? Because the risk's too great. Because not everyone can stop smoking just like that. A half of experimental teen smokers become regular young adult smokers. Half of these young adult smokers smoke till at least retirement age. And even if they can, and do, stop, they won't necessarily 'get away with it'.

Take Christy Turlington, the American supermodel. She smoked up to a pack a day from the age of to 26, with a two-year gap, and enjoyed faultless looks and apparent good health. Five years after quitting, aged only 31, Christy was diagnosed with the chronic lung condition emphysema. She should have been alright. She quit.

Then there's the 1999 study, published in the (American) *Journal of the National Cancer Institute*, which proves that childhood and teenage smoking cause permanent genetic change in the lungs and forever increase the risk of lung cancer.

That study followed Paul Brodish's paper, *The Irreversible Health Effects of Cigarette Smoking*, prepared in 1998 for the American Council on Science and Health. Brodish wrote, 'smoking cigarettes for as few as five years can have a permanent effect on the lungs, the heart, the eyes, the throat, the urinary tract, the digestive organs, the bones and joints, and the skin – even if the smoker quits'.

A Canadian study, which appeared in the *Lancet* in October 2002, shows that girls who start smoking within 5 years of their first menstrual cycle are 80% more likely to develop breast cancer before the age of 50. There's no proof, yet at least, however, that smoking causes breast cancer in adult smokers. So, another specific teen threat.

The cessation world is rightly keen to back the notion that quitting smoking at any age is worthwhile and often uses 'within x days' tables to emphasise the health benefits. The idea that teen and youth smoking can cause permanent damage seems to undermine, and be undermined by, the 'quitting always helps' argument. It doesn't. All it undermines is the idea that smoking only hurts long-term smokers; only kills the old. Christy Turlington's a good contemporary example of a young smoker paying for her one-time habit. But Christy, strangely, is lucky. At least her prognosis is good. Her condition is not, apparently, expected to develop. A closer to home, and scarier, warning was offered in November 2003 by Dr Jesme Baird, Director of Patient Care at the Roy Castle Lung Cancer Foundation.

---

## While, and until, adult smoking is tackled, teenagers will smoke and will do themselves irreparable harm

Dr Baird said, 'A very worrying trend appears to be emerging. What we're hearing from lung cancer consultants across the UK is that the incidence of lung cancer among younger women has been on the increase over the last couple of years. This is a devastating disease and the impact that this must be having on these women, the majority of whom will have young families, is unimaginable.'

Emphysema at 31; lung cancer in 'younger women'. These examples are more likely than images of the 'old' – or middle-aged – struggling with smoking-related disease to worry teenage girl smokers. But they're still abstract. Many teenage smokers live with parents, siblings, uncles and aunts who smoke and enjoy a 'normal', even 'healthy' lifestyle.

Smoking-related disease is most likely to strike grandparents or great-uncles and aunts who, however young in reality, seem ancient. A grandfather's death from lung cancer may devastate his smoking grandson or granddaughter, but won't necessarily dislodge the notion that,

a, he was unlucky, and that, b, he didn't quit in time.

Teenagers, just like adults, know that smoking kills. Most know how it kills. They've heard that it wrecks fitness and skin, too. That it's nigh impossible to quit. But many live with 'happy, healthy' smokers and socialise with smoking friends. They see normal, attractive people smoking everywhere – on the high street, on TV, on the cinema screen.

With this kind of smoking saturation in play, a saturation that implies that the habit is everyday, and must therefore be safe, some experts believe that tackling adult smoking is the key to cutting teen rates. That adult anti-smoking campaigns have a much greater impact on teenagers than teen-specific campaigns and that teenagers won't stop en masse until smoking is not seen as standard adult behaviour.

It's a sound argument. The problem is that while, and until, adult smoking is tackled, teenagers will smoke and will do themselves irreparable harm. Dr David Hill, who champions the 'adult cessation first' approach, writes, 'programmes that increase the proportion of adults giving up smoking will restore to non-smoking status many of those who took up smoking as adolescents, probably with minimal tobacco-related health damage'.

Hmmm. Minimal? He continues: 'I concede that this approach is not an adequate response to the evidence that tobacco exposure during youth may be more harmful, dose for dose, than it is in later life.' So, adult cessation programmes are an answer but not the answer.

Teen-targeted anti-smoking campaigns, rejected by Hill, and by many experts, as at best ineffectual, may even backfire. The tobacco industry is certainly keen to sponsor such initiatives. 'Doesn't Smoke', a £2.4m 2001 campaign, funded by British American Tobacco (BAT), by Philip Morris and by Japan Tobacco International (JTI), and aired on MTV Europe, ran with the aim of 'providing 12 to 17-year-olds with positive non-smoking role models' to spread 'the message that young people can be cool without smoking'. A 2002 Dutch campaign,

'You can be cool and not be a smoker', again sponsored by Philip Morris, pursued the same line. One obvious reading: smoking is cool. An anti-smoking ad? ASH UK have called tobacco-sponsored youth smoking initiatives 'disingenuous, self-serving public relations'.

The tobacco industry backs many other supposedly anti-youth-smoking initiatives. BAT, for example, supports the CitizenCard ID programme, which it claims is meant to cut down underage cigarette sales. BAT has also stated that 'it would be helpful if the UK government were to raise the minimum age for tobacco sales from 16 to 18'. Both approaches, interestingly, promote the 'mature' image of smoking.

One strategy that most experts agree on is the price hike. The World Bank summed up the situation in 1999: 'The most effective way to deter children from smoking is to increase taxes on tobacco. High prices prevent some children and adolescents from starting and en-courage those who already smoke to reduce their consumption.'

ASH agrees. 'Price increases are a concrete, simple, well-documented way to reduce youth smoking rates: this is why the tobacco manufacturers will not campaign for them.'

Another solid strategy is the local, highly tailored approach. QUIT's Break Free programme works with schools to offer students who want to stop smoking a weekly course of seven one-hour support sessions. These sessions are held by a QUIT counsellor who can quickly assess and respond to the needs of the group and of its individual members.

Spending time with teen would-be quitters, listening, and offering thought-out advice and real support, isn't as easy as feeding a 'smoking sucks' one-liner. But that's the point. As QUIT's Chief Executive, Steve Crone, says, 'Break Free support sessions make a very real investment in teenage health. There's no quick fix for teen smoking. That's why we put so much time and expertise into each group, into each student.'

There's hope, then. But, overall, the subject of teenage smoking and cessation is a bit of a downer. A quarter of UK teenagers smoke.

They're doing themselves permanent damage. Whatever their intentions, many won't stop. Education initia-tives, campaigns and policy change can all help. The risks, though, of backfiring, of unwittingly promoting the habit, are huge.

An increase in the number of anti-smoking initiatives targeted at adults, like the British Heart Founda-tion's 'oozing fat' campaign and the smoking bans in Ireland and New York, should herald a fall in adult smoking rates. The effects should, and will, filter down, should alter teenage smoking patterns. That'll take years, though. And we can't afford to write off a generation.

Tax leaps could be one immed-iately effective step. Another could be further investment in tailored, school-based programmes. A co-ordinated approach, which sees carefully form-ulated schemes, and the charities, government bodies and professionals behind them, working in unison, is essential. But there's no easy answer. Especially when 12- and 13-year-old boys tell researchers they smoke because 'we're just the rude boys'.

■ The above article was written by QUIT. For full details of references for this article please contact QUIT on 020 7251 1551 or visit their website at www.quit.org.uk

© QUIT

---

# Chocolate in tobacco 'to attract children'

### By Celia Hall, Medical Editor

**T**obacco companies were accused yesterday of adding food flavours to cigarettes in order to encourage children to start smoking. British American Tobacco said that the flavourings were added to reduce the harshness of tobacco but denied that they were a way of persuading children to smoke.

A list of tobacco additives including food flavours, such as chocolate, sherry, cherry and vanilla, were referred to in a recent research article on the effects that they had on the chemistry of smoke in an experiment with rats.

A BAT spokesman said food flavours had been in cigarettes for many years and the 'recipes' gave cigarettes their flavour. But the tastes could not be identified by the smoker.

Ann Tradigo, a spokesman for BAT, said: 'Ingredients are added but only in very, very minuscule quantities. They are added so the harshness of the tobacco is taken away but you can't taste anything in the cigarettes.'

The company's website shows that brown sugar, liquorice and cocoa extract are added to Lucky Strike sold in Britain. Rothmans Royal 120 has brown sugar in the ingredients.

The company is also allowed to use apple juice, cinnamon bark oil, coffee extract, coriander seed oil, honey, prune extract, red rose oil and vanilla extract.

Amanda Sandford, the research manager for Ash (Action on Smoking and Health), said: 'In the UK 100,000 smokers or people who have smoked die every year and 400,000 give up. They are losing a huge number of customers and the only way to restore their customers is to make sure more children smoke. Making cigarettes less harsh will make them more palatable to children.'

© *Telegraph Group Limited, London 2004*

---

# Children and smoking

## Information from Cancer Research UK

Each day 450 children in the UK take up smoking. Very few 11- and 12-year-old children smoke. However, by the age of 15 years around one in four children in England are regular smokers, despite the fact that it is illegal to sell any tobacco product to people under 16. Since the mid 1980s girls have been more likely to smoke regularly than boys.

Most adult smokers have acquired the habit by the time they are 19, so it seems obvious that efforts to stop children from smoking should focus on school-based education programmes. However it is difficult to find interventions that work with children and simply concentrating on teaching school children that 'smoking is bad for you' is not effective.

### The influence of tobacco advertising

Young people take their role models from a wide range of sources, and research has shown that tobacco advertising is seen by children and influences their smoking behaviour. Tobacco companies have claimed that their advertising is targeted at young adults over the age of 18, but they know that younger teenagers aspire to the older images being portrayed.

Tobacco companies have even designed their own youth anti-smoking campaigns, in an effort to promote themselves as socially responsible. However, strengthening the idea that tobacco use is an adult activity in fact enhances the image of cigarettes as forbidden and smoking as rebellious, and increases the allure of smoking for young teenagers.

It was for this reason that Cancer Research UK and other health organisations lobbied government to introduce legislation banning the use of advertising to promote tobacco products. The Tobacco Advertising and Promotion Act became law in the UK in February 2003 and tobacco cannot now be advertised on billboards, on TV, in the cinema, or in the press. Estimates suggest that this advertising ban will save 3,000 British lives every year – a tremendous victory for public health.

Sponsorship of sporting events has been a particularly powerful way for the tobacco industry to target young people, with its use of dynamic images associated with speed, action and youth. Research funded by Cancer Research UK has shown that tobacco promotion via motor racing impacts on young boys' decisions to take up smoking. Under the new tobacco advertising ban tobacco sponsorship will also be outlawed, but Formula One has until 2006 to find alternative sponsors.

### Anti-smoking campaigns

As the advertising and sponsorship bans come into place, the tobacco industry will need to be more creative in the way they communicate their message, looking at new ways to target potential smokers. Cancer Research UK's researchers at the Centre for Tobacco Control Research in Glasgow will be monitoring the effects of the ban and the tobacco industry's response to it.

As tobacco marketing becomes more sophisticated, anti-smoking campaigns will also need to become more creative. In the US state of Florida a successful approach has been to use a youth-led, youth-marketing approach which exposes the manipulation techniques of the tobacco industry. The TRUTH campaign has, as part of a multi-faceted prevention programme, been very successful in changing young people's attitudes to the tobacco industry and has resulted in decreasing rates of youth smoking.

Children are far more likely to smoke if other people at home smoke. It appears that a sibling smoking has even more influence than a parent smoking. Therefore tobacco education strategies also need to look at adult smoking behaviour. Youth-prevention schemes need to be embedded in a comprehensive programme of advertising bans, adult cessation, taxation and restrictions on smoking at work and in public places.

■ The above information is from Cancer Research UK's website which can be found at www.cancerresearchuk.org

© Cancer Research UK

# Smoking and your health

## Information from the Coronary Prevention Group

Ask most people which illnesses smoking can cause and most of them will answer 'lung cancer'. Over 30,000 people died from lung cancer in 1997 in the UK, and at least 80% of these deaths were due to smoking. But the influence of cigarette smoking on health is much, much wider than this.

Diseases such as bronchitis, emphysema, and circulatory diseases (heart disease, peripheral vascular disease and stroke) are all associated with smoking. These diseases can be fatal, but even when they are not, they will seriously affect quality of life. Circulatory disease can lead to the amputation of limbs, lung diseases can make breathing laborious and painful, and feeling ill for long periods is very unpleasant. Smoking-related diseases can also cost financially as smokers take more time off work due to ill health – British industry loses 50 million working days every year from smoking-related sick leave.

Smoking cigarettes will also change the way you look. Gradually smokers' fingers become stained yellow from the tar, and their hair and complexion seem to lose colour and become greyer. Smokers are also at risk of developing dental disease and bad breath. Not a pretty picture.

### But what is the real risk?

Everybody seems to know somebody who has smoked all their lives but is still as fit as a fiddle. Well they're the (very) lucky ones, as the statistics tell a different story.

- 111,000 people in the UK die from smoking-related diseases every year.
- One in two smokers will die prematurely; 40% of heavy smokers (more than 20 cigarettes a day) die before retirement age, compared to 15% of non-smokers.
- Smoking causes 30,000 deaths a year from heart disease in the UK, and smokers are twice as likely to have a heart attack as non-smokers.
- One-third (46,000) of all cancer deaths in Britain are due to smoking, and lung cancer is the most common cancer in Britain.

### There's no hiding from the facts, it could be you

Women who are taking the oral contraceptive pill are also at greater risk of having a heart attack if they smoke. The increase in risk is tenfold but increases further after the age of 45, so it is very important to give up smoking if you are on the pill.

*One in two smokers will die prematurely; 40% of heavy smokers die before retirement age, compared to 15% of non-smokers*

### Reducing your risk

The good news is that when you stop smoking, all these high risks begin to fall dramatically, and continue to fall as long as you keep away from the cigarettes. Within months your circulation improves and lung function increases by 10%. Five years after quitting and your risk of having a heart attack is half that of a smoker's, and after 10 years, it is the same as a non-smoker's. Risk of lung cancer is also halved after 10 years.

### So why are cigarettes so dangerous?

Cigarettes are a cocktail of literally thousands of chemicals, many of which are toxic or carcinogenic (cancer causing). These chemicals are present in the smoke which both smokers and those around them inhale, and can be gases or tiny solid particles.

Some of the gases in cigarette smoke include carbon monoxide,

---

## What are the risks of continuing to smoke?

### What smoking does to your body

- cancer of the nose
- cancer of the mouth
- increased coughing and sneezing
- shortness of breath
- lung cancer
- leukaemia
- chronic bronchitis and emphysema
- cancer of the kidney
- cancer of the bladder
- affected fertility
- gangrene
- stroke
- defective vision
- cancer of the larynx
- cancer of the throat
- cancer of the oesophagus
- aortic aneurysm
- coronary heart disease
- cancer of the stomach
- peptic ulcer
- cancer of the pancreas
- peripheral vascular disease

*Source: Department of Health, Crown copyright*

ammonia and hydrogen cyanide. The solid particles include nicotine, benzene and tar.

Nicotine is what makes cigarettes so addictive and it is nicotine that your body is craving when you try to give up smoking. The body absorbs nicotine very quickly and it reaches the brain within seconds where its effects cause an increase in blood pressure. Small doses of pure nicotine are fatal.

Carbon monoxide is a poisonous gas which is present in car exhaust fumes and it reduces the blood's ability to carry oxygen (see below).

### Smoking and your heart

The chemicals contained in cigarette smoke affect your heart and circulation in several ways, both immediately and in the long term.

Two immediate effects of lighting up are an increase in your heartbeat rate, and a sharp rise in blood pressure. These responses are caused by nicotine which acts on the nervous system, causing the heart rate to rise and blood vessels to constrict. This narrowing of the blood vessels means that the heart has to pump harder to get blood around the body, thus blood pressure rises and strain is put on the heart.

The carbon monoxide in cigarettes also affects the heart and blood. Normally, oxygen is picked up and carried in the blood by a protein called haemoglobin. If, however, carbon monoxide is present, the haemoglobin will preferentially carry the carbon monoxide, leaving less 'room' for the oxygen. This is bad news for the organs of the body waiting for their oxygen! The oxygen-carrying capacity of a smoker's blood can be cut by up to 15%. Again, this means that the heart has to pump harder to get enough oxygen to the rest of the body.

Smoking can also affect the blood in the longer term. Smokers may have increased blood cholesterol levels, and smoking also changes the way the blood clots. This happens because levels of a protein called fibrinogen are increased and the blood contains more platelets – both these factors mean blood will clot more easily and this will increase the risk of having a heart attack, caused by a blood clot forming in the heart.

Remember though that when you quit smoking, your risk of developing heart disease falls, and many of the changes described above will begin to reverse. You'll be able to breathe more easily and your heart will be able to do its job with much less effort.

■ The above information is from the website www.healthnet.org.uk which is run by the the Coronary Prevention Group

*© The Coronary Prevention Group*

# Smoking and disease

## Information from KATS (Kids against tobacco smoke)

■ The number of people dying each year from smoking-related diseases is equivalent to a jumbo jet crashing every day of the year! That is 330 people each day, 120,000 every year.

■ Approximately half of all regular cigarette smokers will eventually be killed by their habit.

■ The risk of having a heart attack is two or three times greater in smokers than non-smokers.

■ Smoking is the cause of about 90% of peripheral vascular disease which leads to about 2,000 leg amputations each year.

■ Smokers who smoke between 1 and 14 cigarettes a day have 8 times the risk of dying from lung cancer compared to non-smokers. This risk increases the more smoked, with those who smoke over 25 cigarettes a day having 25 times this risk.

■ 30% of all cancer deaths are attributed to smoking.

■ Cancers linked to smoking include lung cancer, cervical cancer, cancers of the mouth, lip and throat, cancer of the pancreas, bladder cancer, stomach cancer, cancer of the kidney and liver cancer.

■ Smoking causes approximately 82% of all deaths from lung cancer, 83% of all deaths from bronchitis and emphysema and about 25% of all deaths from heart disease.

## Why is smoking so harmful?

*Nicotine*
is a highly addictive drug which stimulates the nervous system and causes the heart rate and blood pressure to increase. It also narrows blood vessels and so reduces the blood supply to the heart and the brain. The tightening up of the small blood vessels under the skin causes wrinkles.

*Tar*
is a brown, sticky substance that contains many poisonous chemicals which can cause cancers. Tar gets deposited in the lungs and damages the small hairs (called cilia) which clean the lungs. Tar is also an irritant causing coughing and chronic chest problems.

*Carbon monoxide*
is a poisonous gas with no smell. It is found in car exhaust fumes, leaking gas heaters and burning cigarettes. Carbon monoxide prevents the blood taking up oxygen from the lungs. If you smoke 20 cigarettes a day you will have around 10% less oxygen in your body. This leads to low energy levels, shortness of breath and tiredness. If a smoker is pregnant her baby may not get enough oxygen for healthy growth.

■ The above information is from KATS's web site which can be found at www.roycastle.org/kats/
*© KATS (Kids against tobacco smoke) – The Roy Castle Lung Cancer Foundation*

# Smoking and health

## Information from FOREST

Like the overwhelming majority of smokers, FOREST understands and fully accepts the health risks of smoking and the nature of that risk. Indeed, the health risks have been known for so long (the US Surgeon General first announced a link between smoking and lung cancer in 1964) there cannot be a sane adult in the UK who is not aware of the potential danger.

We do however have a problem with the tactics adopted by politicians and the health industry who routinely use the health argument to say they are 'protecting' smokers from themselves. The health argument is then presented in one of several ways.

The first is to frighten smokers into believing that they will almost certainly die before their time ('Quit or die'). The problem with this message is that it is so obviously false. As a great many families (and even doctors) will testify, many smokers live a long and healthy life, sometimes outliving their non-smoking peers.

Moreover, with one major exception (lung cancer), none of the illnesses described as 'smoking-related' is exclusive to smokers and all are primarily diseases of the elderly. In reality, two-thirds of all deaths in the UK are caused by 'smoking-related diseases', despite the fact that only half of those people actually smoke.

### Other factors

Something else therefore must be causing these 'smoking-related diseases' (and, no, it's not passive smoking!) which is unrelated to smoking – diet, perhaps, or genetic factors, or even general lifestyle (lack of exercise, for example). Or maybe (horror of horrors) it's just old age.

One disease that smoking cannot ignore is lung cancer for the simple reason that it very, very rarely afflicts non-smokers. (The average annual risk of a non-smoker getting lung cancer has been calculated to be 0.01%.) Even for smokers, however, the quit or die message seems a bit excessive. According to Professor Sir Richard Doll (the man who first discovered a correlation between smoking and lung cancer in the 1950s) research suggests that if you start smoking as a teenager and quit aged 30, the risk of developing lung cancer is 2%; give up at 50 and the risk goes up to 8%; give up at 70 (by which time you have been smoking for more than 50 years) and the risk rises to 16%.

Surprised? Let's face it, these figures paint a rather different picture from the anti-smoking lobby which gives the impression that most if not all smokers are going to die a horrible, agonising death well before their time. Again, this isn't to deny the health risks, but let's get this in perspective. In spite of what some people would have you believe, smoking is not a one-way ticket to Death Row.

### Beneficial qualities

Revealingly, the anti-smoking lobby refuses point blank to acknowledge that smoking has any beneficial qualities whatsoever. The health risks of smoking may outweigh the health risks of stress, for example, but there are many smokers who believe passionately that the former helps reduce the latter.

Likewise, many smokers believe (rightly or wrongly) that smoking (and the occasional smoking break) helps improve their concentration and makes them more efficient at work. Meanwhile, instead of welcoming research which suggests that smoking may help ward off Alzheimer's Disease (one of the most debilitating illnesses known to man), the anti-smokers pour scorn on the idea. Why?

Finally, there is a clear lack of perspective in the smoking debate, a factor most clearly illustrated by the anti-smokers' complaint that James Bond, in the 2002 film *Die Another Day*, was seen smoking a cigar (in Cuba!). The fact that they had no problem with 007 having casual, unprotected sex, driving dangerously fast or being in possession of a loaded gun (with intent to kill!) reveals more about their narrow-minded obsession than it does about the dangers of smoking.

■ The above information is from FOREST's website which can be found at www.forestonline.org

*© FOREST*

# Passive smoking may not damage your health

## Passive smoking may not damage your health after all, says research

### By Celia Hall,
### Medical Editor

Passive smoking may not be the killer that many studies have shown, says a study based on the husbands and wives of more than 35,500 smokers.

The research by American researchers attracted a furious response from anti-smoking campaigners who described the paper as misleading and flawed.

The Californian survey, which followed the smokers and their spouses for nearly 40 years, failed to find the increased risk of death from passive smoking associated with coronary heart disease or lung cancer that has been widely reported. However, for the smokers themselves, the risk were clear, they say.

Dr James Enstrom of the school of public health, California University, Los Angeles, and Prof Geoffrey Kabat of the department of preventive medicine, State University of New York, say in the *British Medical Journal*, that the link with passive smoking and diseases 'may be considerably weaker than generally believed'.

Increased risk of lung cancer from passive smoking has been estimated at 20 per cent and, for heart disease, at 30 per cent.

The researchers say: 'Exposure to environmental tobacco smoke could not plausibly cause a 30 per cent increase in risk of coronary heart disease. It seems premature to conclude that environmental tobacco smoke causes death from coronary heart disease and lung cancer.'

The journal refers to possible conflicts of interest. It notes that Dr Enstrom had received funding in recent years from the tobacco industry because 'it has been impossible for him to obtain equivalent funds from other sources'.

Prof Kabat never received tobacco-related money until last year when he carried out a review for a law firm which had tobacco companies as clients. The journal says: 'Both are lifelong non-smokers whose primary interest is an accurate determination of the health effects of tobacco.'

The journal also published a commentary on the Californian study by George Davey Smith, professor of clinical epidemiology, Bristol University, who says the researchers may have 'over-emphasised' the negative nature of their findings.

> ### 'The debate on environmental tobacco smoke is far from over, contrary to what many people say

Despite this it is certain this paper will be hailed as showing that the detrimental effect of passive smoking has been overstated and the controversy will continue.

Doreen McIntyre, chief executive of No Smoking Day, said the study was highly misleading. 'This paper is disingenuous and a real insult to the thousands of people suffering and dying every day from tobacco smoke, particularly those dying from other people's tobacco smoke.'

Amanda Sandford, research manager of Ash (Action on Smoking and Health), said the paper was 'just the latest in a long campaign to sow seeds of doubt about the dangers of breathing in environmental tobacco smoke'.

The British Thoracic Society said the paper was 'yet another piece of evidence in the difficult debate on passive smoking'.

Dr Ian Campbell, its president, said: 'There are real risks involved which need to be addressed.' Conclusive evidence showed passive smoking had a detrimental effect on children's lungs, he said, and there was good evidence to suggest it worsened the effects of asthma.

FOREST, the smokers' lobby group, welcomed the study.

Dr Vivienne Nathanson, head of science and ethics at the British Medical Association, said it would be 'wrong to be swayed by one flawed study funded by the tobacco industry – set against the studies and numerous expert reviews that demonstrate that passive smoking kills'.

Tim Lord, chief executive of the Tobacco Manufacturers' Association, said: 'The debate on environmental tobacco smoke is far from over, contrary to what many people say.

'Taking the evidence as a whole, the inevitable conclusion is that claims made about the potentially harmful effects of passive smoking have indeed been overstated.'

He said non-smokers should have access to clean air and smokers should behave with consideration towards others. But he added: 'What is quite clear from this latest study is that the body of scientific evidence certainly does not justify total bans on smoking in the workplace or other public places.'

Earlier this week the NHS Smoking Helpline reported that more than 10,000 people wanting to stop had made contact in the first four months of this year in response to the new, graphic 'smoking kills' warnings on cigarette packets – an increase of 12 per cent in calls to the helpline.

# Double the danger for passive smokers

The risks of heart disease faced by passive smokers are double what was previously estimated, a study revealed today (30 June 2004).

Previous research has found that passive smoking is linked with a 25-30% increased risk of coronary heart disease.

But the latest study, published on bmj.com, found that non-smokers faced a 50-60% increased risk of falling victim to the disease.

The researchers noted that most studies on passive smoking examined the risks of living with someone who smoked.

### Additional exposure

They said while this was important it did not take into account the additional exposure at work and other places like pubs and restaurants.

The team said that by measuring cotinine – a by-product of nicotine – they could get a more accurate measure of exposure to smoke from all sources.

The study focused on 4,792 men from 18 British towns who were monitored for 20 years.

The researchers took blood samples to measure cotinine, concluding that higher concentrations in the blood of non-smokers were associated with a 50-60% greater risk of heart disease.

### Increased risks

They said that the risks were increased in the early follow-up period, indicating that the link between cotinine levels and heart disease seemed to decline with time.

This suggested another source of underestimation of the effects of passive smoking because other studies have had much longer follow-up periods.

The researchers said more studies were needed to find the link between cotinine and other biomarkers and the increased risk of heart disease to help assess the impact of passive smoking.

Researcher Prof Peter Whincup, of the Department of Community Health Sciences at St George's Hospital Medical School in London, highlighted the case for tackling passive smoking.

'This study adds to the weight of evidence that passive smoking is harmful and strengthens the case for limiting exposure to passive smoking as much as we can.'

### Lower levels of second-hand smoke

He added: 'People are smoking less now so non-smokers are exposed to lower levels of second-hand smoke.

'But this study suggests the harmful effects of passive smoking have been underestimated in the past because previous studies only looked at the effect of a non-smoker living with a partner who smoked.

'They gave a 25-30% increased risk.

'Using a biological marker for passive smoking allowed us to assess the effect of wider exposure on heart disease risk.'

Deborah Arnott, director of anti-smoking campaign group ASH, said: 'This important study provides yet more evidence of the serious health risks posed by second-hand smoke.

'It suggests that if you regularly breathe in other people's smoke at home or at work your chances of getting heart disease may rise by more than a half.

'This is a much bigger increase in risk than was previously thought – and the difference with previous estimates seems mainly due to smoking in the workplace.'

### Calls for a smoking ban

She again called for the Government to ban smoking in public places in the light of all the evidence on the dangers of second-hand smoke.

Dr Tim Bowker, associate medical director of the British Heart Foundation, said: 'The need for a ban on smoking in public places in the UK has never been better illustrated than by this potentially pivotal study.

'We have known for some time that passive smoking was strongly associated with increased risk of coronary heart disease, but this study strengthens the evidence considerably.'

He added: 'To think that people who choose not to smoke can suffer an increased risk of CHD of around 50% just by frequenting smoky public places is disturbing.

'The evidence is now compelling.

'The Government should not delay any further in introducing legislation to protect non-smokers from this unnecessary risk.'

■ This article first appeared in the *Daily Mail*, 30 June, 2004.

# Smoking and cancer

## Information from Cancer Research UK

### Key facts

- Tobacco is the leading preventable cause of cancer worldwide.
- One-third of the 151,000 cancer deaths each year in the UK are estimated to be the result of smoking.[1]
- Smoking causes 120,000 deaths in the UK each year from diseases including cancers, heart disease and stroke.[2]

### Tobacco as a cause of death

Lung cancer is the commonest cancer worldwide, with over one million new cases every year.[3] It is the second most common cancer in the UK (after breast cancer). Tobacco smoking causes around nine out of ten cases of lung cancer in the UK.

In 1998, 38,780 people in the UK were diagnosed with lung cancer.[4,5,6,7]

On average in the UK, 92 people die from lung cancer every day – one person every 15 minutes.[8,9,10]

Several hundred people also die every year from lung cancer caused by passive smoking – breathing other people's tobacco smoke.[11]

Many other cancers have been linked to tobacco consumption and those estimated to be substantially caused by smoking include cancers of the upper respiratory tract (lip, tongue, mouth, voice-box [larynx], throat ]pharynx]), bladder, pancreas, food pipe (oesophagus), stomach, kidney and leukaemia. An increased risk for cancer of the cervix has also been linked to smoking.[12, 13]

Besides the cancer death toll, most deaths from chronic bronchitis and emphysema and a quarter of all heart disease deaths are the result of smoking.[2]

### The risks

Tobacco has no safe level of use. Overall, one in two smokers (smoking 20 a day from age 18) will die from their habit – half of them in middle age.[14]

- Risk is directly related to the number of cigarettes smoked – the higher the consumption, the greater the risk.
- Risk is even more dependent on duration of smoking than on consumption. For example, smoking one packet of cigarettes a day for 40 years is eight times more hazardous than smoking two packets a day for 20 years.[15]
- Ceasing to smoke reduces risk. Smokers who stop before age 35 have a life expectancy not significantly different from non-smokers, while stopping in middle age, before the onset of cancer or some other serious disease, avoids most of the later excess risk from tobacco.[16] Staying off cigarettes for ten years probably halves the risk of lung cancer. The longer you stop, the lower the risk.[17]

### The global picture

- There are 1.1 billion smokers in the world.[18]
- There will be 1,000 million (1 billion) tobacco deaths worldwide in the 21st century if current global smoking patterns continue – a tenfold increase on the 20th-century toll of 100 million.[15]
- By the year 2030 the worldwide number of tobacco-related deaths each year will increase from 4 to 10 million. 80 per cent of them will occur in developing countries.[19, 20]

### Adult smoking habits in the UK

British men began to smoke cigarettes at the turn of the century and after the Second World War smoking was extremely prevalent. At this time, eight out of ten men smoked some form of tobacco. By 1970 the percentage of men smoking had fallen to 55 per cent. From the 1970s onwards, the numbers fell rapidly and in 2000 less than three out of ten men were smokers.[15,21]

Smoking was not a common habit in women until after the Second World War. The proportion of women smoking cigarettes remained remarkably constant (about four out of ten) between 1948 and 1970, while the proportion of male smokers fell. Consumption in women has since declined, although by a smaller proportion than for men. Between 1978 and 1998 the number of men smoking decreased by 16 per cent, and that of women by 10 per cent.[21,22,23]

In Britain today around a quarter of the adult population – 15 million people – smoke. Smoking is most common in young people, with 40% of men and 35% of women aged 25-34 smoking regularly.[23]

### Children and smoking

Each day 450 children in the UK take up smoking.[24] Most adult smokers have acquired the habit by the time they are 19, so preventing children from starting to smoke is vital.

Very few 11- and 12-year-old children smoke, but by the age of 15 years, around 1 in 4 children are regular smokers in England despite the fact that it is illegal to sell any tobacco product to people under 16. At 15 years of age, 21 per cent of boys and 26 per cent of girls are regular smokers. Since the mid 1980s girls have been more likely than boys to smoke regularly.[25]

Children are far more likely to smoke if other people at home smoke. Siblings smoking appears to have even more influence than a parent smoking. Research has also shown that tobacco advertising influences young people to start smoking.[26]

### Lung cancer rates in the UK

The numbers of new cases of lung cancer in any given year reflect the past smoking habits of men and women. In men, lung cancer rates have been decreasing since the 1970s, about 20 years after the decline in the numbers of men smoking. In women, lung cancer rates increased until the early 1990s and then reached a plateau. This is consistent with women taking up smoking in large numbers later than men and the numbers of female smokers levelling off around the 1970s.

## Global trends

The UK and the USA have among the highest rates of lung cancer in women in the world at present. However, both countries have the fastest falling rates of lung cancer in men.[28]

While the peak levels for lung cancer in men have come and gone in this country, the peak for women is still with us. It has yet to be reached in countries where women took up smoking more recently. UK women have been smoking in greater numbers for much longer than women in most of the rest of Europe, and are five times more likely to die from lung cancer than women in Spain, and four times more likely than women in Portugal and France. Denmark is the only European country that has higher rates of lung cancer in women than the UK.[15]

Of the EU countries, Greece has the highest rate of smoking in men (46%) and Sweden the lowest (22%). Among women, Ireland has the highest rate of smoking (31%) and Portugal the lowest (7%). Worldwide, the vast majority of smokers are in Asia (54.5%).[29]

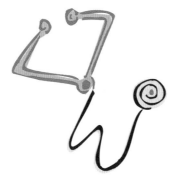

### References

1 *Nicotine Addiction in Britain.* A report of the Tobacco Advisory Group of the RCP. RCP. (2000)

2 Ash Basic Facts No 2. Smoking and disease www.ash.org.uk (2002)

3 Ferlay J, Bray F, Pisani P and Parkin DM. Globocan 2000. *Cancer Incidence, Mortality and Prevalence Worldwide,* Version 1.0. IARC Cancerbase No 5. Lyon, IARC Press (2000).

4 Cancer Statistics Registrations; England, Series MB2, National Statistics (2002)

5 Cancer Incidence in Wales 1989-1998 (2001), Welsh Cancer Intelligence and Surveillance Unit

6 ISD Online: www.show.scot.nhs.uk/

isd/cancer/facts figures/types.lung.htm

7 Cancer Incidence Data 1993-1996 and Mortality Data 1993-1996, Northern Ireland Cancer Registry (2000)

8 Office for National Statistics Series DH2 No 26. *Mortality Statistics: Cause.* England and Wales 2000. TSO (2002)

9 Registrar General for Scotland, Annual Report 2000. GRO for Scotland (2001)

10 Registrar General for Northern Ireland, Annual Report 2000. GRO for Northern Ireland (2001)

11 ASH Factsheet No 8: Passive Smoking www.ash.org.uk (2002)

12 Doll R. Cancers weakly related to smoking. *Br Med Bull* 52, 35-49

13 CRC CancerStats: Cervical cancer (2000)

14 Peto R. Smoking and death: the past 40 years and the next 40. *BMJ* 309, 937-939 (1994)

15 CRC CancerStats: Lung cancer and smoking – UK (June 2001)

16 Peto R, Darby S, Deo H et al. Smoking, smoking cessation and lung cancer in the UK since 1950: combination of national statistics with the case-control studies. *BMJ* 321, 323-9 (2000)

17 Peto R, Lopez AD. The future worldwide health effects of current smoking patterns. In *Global Health in the 21st Century.* Jossey-Bass (2000)

18 World Bank. *Curbing the Epidemic: governments and the economics of tobacco control.* (1999)

19 World Bank *World Development Indicators.* World Bank (1998)

20 Murray C, Lopez A. *The Global Burden of Disease: A Comprehensive Assessment of Mortality and Disability from Disease, Injuries and Risk Factors in 1990 and Projected to 2020.* (1990)

21 Wald N and Nicolaides-Bouman A. *UK Smoking Statistics.* Second Edition. OUP (1991)

22 Office of National Statistics. *Living in Britain: Results from the 1998 General Household Survey.* TSO (2000)

23 Office of National Statistics. *Smoking Related Behaviour and Attitudes, 1999.* TSO (2000)

24 ASH Factsheet No 3. *Young People and Smoking.*

25 Drug Use, Smoking and Drinking among Young People in England in 2000 www.doh.gov.uk/public/sddsurveynov01.htm (2001)

26 MacFadyen L, Hastings G, MacKintosh AM. Cross sectional study of young people's awareness of and involvement with tobacco marketing. *BMJ* (2001) Mar 3, 322 (7285): 513-7

27 Parkin DM, Whelan SL, Ferlay J et al. *Cancer Incidence in Five Continents* Vol VII. IARC Scientific Publications No 143: Lyons (1997)

28 Peto R and Doll R. Figures presented at UICC 18th International Cancer Congress, Oslo (July 2002)

29 http://tobaccofreekids.org/campaign/global/factsheets.html

© *Cancer Research UK*

## Lung cancer

### Cases diagnosed and age-standardised incidence rates for lung cancer, per 100,000 population, UK 2000

|  | England | Wales | Scotland | N. Ireland | UK |
|---|---|---|---|---|---|
| **Cases** | | | | | |
| Males | 19,035 | 1,267 | 2,446 | 497 | 23,245 |
| Females | 12,055 | 817 | 1,948 | 345 | 15,165 |
| Total | 31,090 | 2,084 | 4,394 | 842 | 38,410 |
| **Rates** | | | | | |
| Males | 67.4 | 70.4 | 87.8 | 63.2 | 69.2 |
| Females | 34.0 | 36.5 | 51.8 | 35.0 | 35.8 |
| Total | 48.3 | 50.9 | 66.7 | 46.9 | 50.0 |

Source: Cancer Research UK

**Issues**

*www.independence.co.uk*

# Smokers at cancer risk even after cutting back

**By Robin Yapp,
Science Reporter**

Smokers were warned yesterday that cutting down on cigarettes is not enough to protect them against cancer.

People who smoke more than a pack a day and then reduce their consumption by around 90 per cent, experience a fall of only half that much in the level of cancer-causing chemicals in their body, according to a study.

Researchers believe that when smokers try to cut back they experience withdrawal symptoms and so inhale longer and deeper on the few cigarettes they do smoke.

Lung cancer is the biggest cancer killer in the UK, causing more than 33,000 deaths every year – more than twice as many as bowel cancer, the next most deadly form of the disease.

Around 38,000 cases of lung cancer are diagnosed annually – 90 per cent of them caused by cigarettes – and only 5 per cent of victims live for more than five years.

In the latest study, scientists at the University of Minnesota studied a group of 153 heavy smokers, 102 of whom were asked to gradually cut down on cigarettes over several weeks.

Dr Stephen Hecht and colleagues measured the levels of NNK – a cancer-causing chemical unique to tobacco – in urine samples before the study began and then on a weekly basis.

Smokers who had reduced their cigarette consumption by nearly two-thirds (63 per cent) by week 12 experienced a drop of only 28 per cent in NNK levels in their system.

Those who had managed to cut down by 74 per cent fared little better with a reduction of just 29 per cent.

The story was little better for the smokers who had cut down the most – from an average of 25 cigarettes a day before the study began to just 2.6 per day on average by week 12.

This 90 per cent reduction in cigarettes smoked produced only a 46 per cent decrease in traces of cancer-causing substances recorded.

Such smokers were therefore gaining 4.3 times more NNK per cigarette than before the study, reported the *Journal of the National Cancer Institute* 21 January 2004.

> *Around 38,000 cases of lung cancer are diagnosed annually – 90 per cent of them caused by cigarettes – and only 5 per cent of victims live for more than five years*

Dr Hecht said that the most likely explanation is that smokers took larger puffs and shorter intervals between puffs to 'compensate' for the cutback in cigarettes.

'The results indicate that some smokers may benefit from reduced smoking, but for most the effects are modest,' he said.

Scott Leischow, of the US National Cancer Institute, said: 'Given the dearth of evidence supporting the benefits of reduced smoking, and given the strong evidence that smoking cessation can have a dramatic impact on future tobacco-related mortality, the most dramatic health benefits will occur if we can significantly increase the number of smokers who quit.'

Dr Marcus Munafo, a scientist with Cancer Research UK, said: 'People are addicted to nicotine and if they cut down on cigarettes they just seems to suck harder and make more of each one.

'The basic message must be there is no substitute for stopping altogether, and the sooner the better because it takes ten years after quitting for the risk of heart disease to return to that of a non-smoker and 15-20 years for the risk of lung cancer.'

# Smoke screen

**Passive smoking at work kills three workers in Britain every day, according to a new report. Medical experts, unions, public health specialists and workers want this deadly hazard outlawed. The tobacco and hospitality industries do not. Guess who the government is listening to?**

E very year 1,200 people in the UK – three a day – die due to passive smoking at work, according to new research by second-hand smoke expert James Repace.

*A killer on the loose* reveals that in the UK around 900 office workers, 165 bar workers and 145 manufacturing workers die each year as a direct result of breathing in other people's tobacco smoke at work.

The figures show that there are three times as many deaths a year from passive smoking at work as from workplace injuries. ASH research suggests three million people in the UK are exposed to second-hand smoke while at work.

James Repace said: 'This study shows that previous research has seriously under-estimated the number of people killed by second-hand smoke at work.'

The TUC, Action on Smoking and Health (ASH) and the Chartered Institute of Environmental Health (CIEH), who teamed up for a 9 April 'Don' t choke on the smoke' conference, say the research demonstrates the need for a legally binding Code of Practice for workplace smoking, proposed over two years ago by the Health and Safety Commission.

Amanda Sandford of the anti-tobacco campaigning group ASH said: 'One death caused by passive smoking is unacceptable but more than 1,000 a year is a disgrace and for every day's delay the government has deaths on its conscience.'

## Why won't they act?

ASH has accused the government of being more concerned with keeping the tobacco and hospitality industries happy than it is with keeping the workforce healthy.

In March, ASH charged the government with suppressing a study that concluded thousands of lives

*By Rory O'Neill*

and millions in business and health care costs could be saved each year by outlawing smoking at work.

The unpublished HSC study says up to 2,340 lives a year could be saved by banning workplace smoking. The total savings to government and business, including the National Health Service, could be £21 billion, the study says.

*'This study shows that previous research has seriously under-estimated the number of people killed by second-hand smoke at work'*

ASH says the government is 'putting the inflated concerns of the hospitality trade and small businesses ahead of the very real health impact of passive smoking'.

Internal industry documents show that tobacco manufacturers have deliberately conspired to prevent bars and restaurants from becoming smoke-free zones.

Researchers writing in the June 2002 issue of the medical journal *Tobacco Control* say the evidence that profits would be hit was a tobacco industry smoke screen and the industry had in fact conned the hospitality trade, which the industry says 'is our greatest potential ally', into doing its dirty work.

## Making a packet

The authors say tobacco manufacturers gave donations to hospitality groups as part of an 'aggressive and effective worldwide campaign to recruit hospitality associations' in

the USA and Europe – including groups dedicated to lobbying the European Commission. Where these associations didn't exist, it created its own front organisations.

This strategy went beyond hospitality organisations. The paper points out 'a programme in the UK titled, "The Atmosphere Improves Results (AIR)" initiative, launched in 1997, received funding from the national tobacco manufacturers' association'.

London-based AIR is still active today. One non-operational page on its website www.airinitiative.com is the 'who's signing up?' page. AIR' s 'avoid legislation' webpage, however, is fully operational and says: 'In other parts of the world where tough legislation has been imposed the hospitality industry has been hit hard. Restaurants, bars and pubs have experienced falling turnover and have had to make staff cuts. Some have even been forced to close.'

The *Tobacco Control* paper concludes: 'Through the myth of lost profits, the tobacco industry has fooled the hospitality industry into embracing expensive ventilation equipment, while in reality 100 per cent smoke-free laws have been shown to have no effect on business revenues, or even to improve them.'

## The smoking gun

A new study in *Tobacco Control*, published in March 2003, has confirmed the positive impact of smoking bans on hospitality venues.

An analysis of 97 studies in eight countries on the impact of smoking bans on the hospitality industry showed that the most rigorous and independent studies found no negative impact on business.

Researchers found that those studies that concluded smoking bans were bad for business were poor quality. They were four times as likely to use subjective rather than objective measures to estimate the impact and 20 times less likely to be peer reviewed.

All the studies that concluded smoking bans had a negative impact were funded by sources that were in some way related to the tobacco industry.

Of the 21 quality studies, none reported a negative impact on business, and four reported that bans had a positive effect.

The US experience suggests the tobacco industry is playing for time – once bans are implemented, hospitality employers quickly come to appreciate them. And their customers like them too.

The April 2003 edition of the *American Journal of Public Health* reports a study in California, which has had workplace no-smoking rules for eight years, which found most bar-goers said they supported and complied with a similar law two years after it went into effect. While 60 per cent approved of the law three months after it went into effect, that number reached 73 per cent about 2.5 years after the law was in place.

Brendan Barber, who steps up from the post of deputy to general secretary of the TUC in June, said: 'Ministers should stop defending the fug-filled snugs of Britain's pubs, which are proving fatal for bar staff and putting off possible customers.

'The Code of Practice is sensible and pragmatic, and it's backed by unions and employers. It will protect the rights of non-smokers and smokers alike, and will end the uncertainty about where employers stand.'

CIEH president Brian Hanna, who represents the health inspectors who would enforce the code in service sector workplaces – such as offices, hotels, pubs and clubs – said inspectors 'need the government to provide them with the right tools to do the job. Relying on weak voluntary arrangements will simply not have the desired effect.'

*A killer on the loose*, the ASH investigation into the threat of passive smoking to the UK work-force, April 2003.
*Passive smoking at work: The global pressure mounts*, Rory O'Neill

## Strong support for workplace smoking law

**There is considerable public demand for a ban on smoking in workplaces according to this MORI survey for public health charity Action on Smoking and Health (ASH).**

**Q. Which of the following statements best applies to you?**

| | |
|---|---|
| I have never smoked | 45% |
| I used to smoke but have given up now | 26% |
| I smoke but I don't smoke every day | 5% |
| I smoked every day | 24% |
| Don't know | * |

**Q. How strongly, if at all, do you agree or disagree with the following statement about smoking in the workplace? 'All employees should have the right to work in a smoke-free environment.'**

| | |
|---|---|
| Strongly agree | 65% |
| Tend to agree | 24% |
| Neither agree nor disagree | 5% |
| Tend to disagree | 3% |
| Strongly disagree | 2% |
| Don't know | * |

**Q. Ireland, Canada, Norway and New Zealand have each passed laws to ensure all enclosed workplaces are smoke free. How strongly, if at all, would you support or oppose a proposal to bring in a similar law in this country?**

| | |
|---|---|
| Strongly support a smoke free law | 54% |
| Tend to support | 25% |
| Neither support nor oppose | 8% |
| Tend to oppose | 7% |
| Strongly oppose a smoke free law | 4% |
| Don't know | * |

**Q. How strongly do you feel, if at all, you would support or oppose a law to make the following places smoke free?**

| | Strongly support | Tend to support | Neither support nor oppose | Tend to oppose | Strongly oppose | Don't know |
|---|---|---|---|---|---|---|
| Enclosed shopping centres and shopping malls | 57% | 29% | 7% | 5% | 2% | * |
| Cafes | 53% | 25% | 9% | 10% | 3% | * |
| NHS hospitals and clinics | 84% | 12% | 2% | 1% | 1% | * |
| Restaurants | 57% | 22% | 9% | 9% | 3% | * |
| Pubs and bars | 30% | 19% | 16% | 22% | 12% | 1% |
| Major railway stations | 38% | 24% | 19% | 14% | 5% | 1% |
| Nightclubs | 30% | 17% | 18% | 21% | 12% | 3% |

*Source: MORI*

and Owen Tudor, TUC, April 2003. www.tuc.org.uk/risks

S Glantz and others. Tobacco industry manipulation of the hospitality industry to maintain smoking in public places, *Tobacco*

---

*Ministers should stop defending the fug-filled snugs of Britain's pubs, which are proving fatal for bar staff and putting off possible customers'*

---

*Control*, vol. 11. pages 94-104, June 2002. www.tobaccocontrol.com

M Scollo, A Lal, A Hyland, S Glantz. Review of the quality of studies on the economic effects of smoke-free policies on the hospitality industry, *Tobacco Control*, vol. 12, pages 13-20, March 2003.

Hao Tang and others. Changes of attitudes and patronage behaviours in response to a smoke-free bar law, *American Journal of Public Health*, vol. 93, pages 611-617, 2003.

■ The above article is from *Hazards*. For more information visit www.hazards.org

© *Hazards Publications Ltd*

# Ban smoking in public, say top doctors

*By Celia Hall,*
*Medical Editor*

Britain's most senior doctors called yesterday for a ban on smoking in public places. They estimate that it could save 160,000 lives.

The unprecedented call from all 13 royal medical colleges and five medical faculties says most people in Britain are now non-smokers and find cigarette smoke unpleasant and irritating.

'We believe the time has come for legislation to make public places smoke-free. All have a right to freedom from tobacco smoke and pollution,' the doctors said.

They say 1,000 people die each year from passive smoking, which also causes asthma, lung infections and middle ear disease in children.

But the Government encourages voluntary bans at work and in pubs and clubs and Melanie Johnson, the minister for public health, said 26 November 2003, that outlawing smoking in public places would be premature.

'Smoke-free places are the ideal but the evidence is that public opinion remains divided. There is also cost and a difficulty involved in enforcing a smoking ban.

'We are calling on the hospitality industry to deliver faster and more substantial improvements in providing smoke-free environments.

'The ban idea is still premature because we do need to take people with us. There is a great deal more to be done by way of public persuasion and education and there would be problems if we had a ban with enforcement.

'If you have people deciding to light up in certain places, you cannot have a policeman standing at their shoulder all the time.'

The call was led by the Royal College of Physicians, which began calling for restricting smoking in public places 43 years ago.

Prof Carol Black, royal college president, said: 'In 1998 the Government said there was no doubt smoking kills and suggested progress could be achieved by working with [the tobacco] industry rather than to enforce a public ban.

'That progress has not been fast,' she said.

A letter published in *The Times* newspaper argues that preventing smoking in the workplace would save about 160,000 lives over time.

'Many workplaces are now smoke-free but in the hospitality industry smoke exposure is still very high and poses a particular risk,' the letter also says.

## 'We believe the time has come for legislation to make public places smoke-free'

'The current system of self-regulation has failed to protect the majority of staff or customers,' it adds.

Dr John Britton, chairman of the college's tobacco advisory group, said the number of lives that could be saved was based on the four per cent who are estimated to stop smoking in workplaces when bans are introduced.

'It has been estimated that about 320,000 people would stop smoking over a period of time and we know that about half of smokers die prematurely,' Dr Britton said.

A spokesman for the Department of Health said progress was being made in voluntary smoking bans and a survey had shown that 50 per cent still wanted to be able to choose to smoke in pubs.

'We are pursuing a voluntary ban. People have a right to choose and businesses respond to customer and consumer demand.' He said Pizza Hut had introduced a ban this year based on what staff and customers wanted.

'In 1996 40 per cent of workplaces had smoke-free policies and this has risen to 50 per cent by 2002. There is progress. The Government has spent £31 million on advertising advising people not to smoke. But at the same time we are aware that people have a right to choose.'

Anti-smoking group Ash welcomed the letter. 'It's a very important move,' said Amanda Sandford. 'We are very pleased that the Colleges have done this. The more pressure we have on the Government the better.'

The British Lung Foundation also welcomed the call. 'The damage to lungs from second-hand smoke has long been acknowledged and the charity thinks it is vital that people protect themselves from these dangers.

'More than eight million people have a lung condition in Britain and all of them are severely aggravated by exposure to second-hand smoke.

'People should have the right to be able to work without being exposed to dangers to their health.'

The call comes only months after the Government's chief medical officer recommended the outlawing of smoking in bars, pubs, clubs and restaurants. Sir Liam Donaldson said a complete ban in public places would reduce dramatically lung cancer, heart disease, bronchitis, pneumonia and asthma caused by passive smoking.

Tim Lord, chief executive of the Tobacco Manufacturers' Association, said there was confusion over what the public wanted.

'While Prof Black et al state that the majority of smokers and non-smokers would prefer public places not to be smoke free, what they fail to acknowledge is the progress that has already been made.

'The public has a very common-sense attitude to smoking in hospitality outlets.'

# What people really think about public smoking

## Information from the Tobacco Manufacturers' Association

### What people really think

#### Introduction

Should smoking in clubs, pubs, bars and restaurants be banned? Some say yes and they have been most forceful in promoting their views. So what do the public and those who use these venues really think?

There have been conflicting claims about what people really want. Some of these claims seem to be based on 'research' that is, frankly, poorly conducted and unreliable.

So the Tobacco Manufacturers' Association (TMA) decided to find out how the general public really do feel about the current situation. This article outlines the results of recent quantitative research which shows where public smoking stands on most people's list of priorities, and what they would like to see happen next.

#### What do the public really think?

The British public shows few signs of wanting to follow the New York model of banishing smokers from restaurants and bars. We have carried out independent research revealing an altogether more moderate and pragmatic attitude. The majority favour practical measures to reduce exposure to other people's smoke rather than an outright ban on smoking.

### Research results

#### Smoking in pubs, clubs and bars

- Three out of ten non-smokers (30 per cent) and over half of adult smokers (55 per cent) have no real concern about smoking in pubs, clubs and bars.
- Less than a fifth (17 per cent) of all adults agree that smoking should be banned in pubs, clubs and bars.
- The great majority (86 per cent) feel that the smoking situation in pubs, clubs and bars has improved in recent years, with almost three-

tobacco manufacturers' association

quarters (73 per cent) noting that the number of non-smoking areas has increased.

- Most people (75 per cent) feel more improvements are still needed but requiring good ventilation is a more popular option (24 per cent) than banning smoking (17 per cent), increasing the number of non-smoking areas (16 per cent) or banning smoking at the bar (4 per cent).

#### Smoking in restaurants

- There is stronger support for smoking restrictions in restaurants than in pubs.
- But still only a third feel it should be banned altogether (32 per cent) or in other places where food is served (14 per cent).
- Many prefer a more flexible approach, the most popular options being more non-smoking areas (19 per cent), offering a real choice of smoking policies (10 per cent) or leaving it up to the management (8 per cent).

#### Other priorities

- Top of the public's list of quality of life issues on which they think local authorities should concentrate resources was 'controlling yobbish behaviour' (37 per cent), followed by 'increasing security camera surveillance' (19 per cent). Even 'maintaining parks and open spaces' (18 per cent) and 'prohibiting litter and graffiti' (12 per cent) were of greater concern than banning smoking (9%), with only 'banning cars from city centres' ranking lower (3 per cent).

#### Smoking in pubs, clubs and bars…

86% feel the situation has improved in recent years.

73% note that the number of non-smoking areas has increased.

#### Smoking in restaurants…

67% want more restrictions but not a complete ban.

#### Other priorities for local authorities…

37% want to ban yobbish behaviour.

9% want to ban smoking.

### The Government's view

Responding to calls for a ban, Public Health Minister Melanie Johnson MP said that a ban would be 'premature' and that more still needs to be done by way of 'public persuasion'. In January 2004, Culture Secretary Tessa Jowell MP said she wanted the hospitality industry to improve conditions voluntarily rather than have a smoking ban imposed.

### The hospitality industry

The Charter Group (consisting of 15 trade associations which represent over 100,000 pubs, clubs, hotels and restaurants) supports a Public Places Charter on smoking.

The Public Places Charter is a voluntary code, agreed with the

Government, to improve choice. It allows customers to know whether they can smoke in a venue, and whether it has non-smoking and ventilated areas. It was included in outline in the 'Smoking Kills' White Paper in December 1998 and formally launched in September 1999 by Tessa Jowell, then Minister for Public Health. According to a 2003 independent validation report commissioned in partnership with the Department of Health, 63% of pubs now carry external policy signage and over half of these have smoking bans, non-smoking areas and/or high quality ventilation.

### What do we think?

The Tobacco Manufacturers' Association believes that the available evidence on the possible health effects of environmental tobacco smoke does not justify calls for a total ban on smoking in public. This would be an unnecessary limitation of choice and personal freedom.

The TMA supports voluntary health and safety measures in work and public places to ensure employees work in well-ventilated, non-smoky air. Clear smoking policies should be established and there should be provision of effective ventilation and facilities for both smokers and non-smokers. There is no need for a legislative ban on smoking in the workplace because voluntary self-regulation is working.

The TMA's chief executive, Tim Lord, commented that the survey shows 'the British public has a very practical, commonsense attitude to smoking in hospitality outlets, preferring to accommodate smokers and non-smokers where possible. Most people have noticed the improvements in pubs and bars and believe more of the same is the most sensible course. The majority do not support a ban, and most seem to feel that further improvements can be achieved on a voluntary basis rather than through regulation.'

### How was the research carried out?

The survey was commissioned by the Tobacco Manufacturers' Association and carried out by BMRB International, using its weekend telephone omnibus survey ACCESS. 1,929 adults aged over 18 were interviewed in September 2003. BMRB used a nationally representative survey and standard sampling techniques rather than some web-based polling which may be open to manipulation and cannot guarantee representative samples.

■ The above information is from a report by the Tobacco Manufacturers' Association. For further details visit their website at www.the-tma.org.uk

© Tobacco Manufacturers' Association

# Fight for choice

**Smokers' lobby group launches major campaign urging Britain to 'fight for choice'. New poll reveals 74% do NOT support smoking ban in pubs, clubs and bars**

Smokers' lobby group FOREST is today announcing a national 'Fight for Choice' campaign designed to highlight the threat of a New York style smoking ban. The campaign will include press advertisements, posters and direct mail.

The 'Smoke Police' advertisement, which launches this week in national magazines and regional newspapers, offers an alarming picture of what the future might hold for smokers if a ban on smoking in pubs was brought in.

To tie in with the launch, a new independent Populus poll of 10,000 people in ten regions across Britain has also been carried out and the findings show that seven out of ten people (74%) do not support a ban on smoking in pubs and bars.

The comprehensive, regionally representative survey found that only 24% of people thought smoking should be banned completely in pubs, clubs and bars, and almost two-thirds

(63%) said policies on smoking should be left to the owners and managers of individual premises, rather than central government (14%) or local councils (21%).

The survey also found that the British public agreed that a ban could harm the atmosphere of pubs, clubs and bars and prove divisive, as smokers and non-smokers would be forced to socialise separately. A majority of respondents agreed that environments have significantly improved, are noticeably less smoky, and that the number of smoking areas and venues has increased.

Less than one person in six (15%) thought that banning smoking in public places should be the highest priority of their local council for improving the quality of life locally. Controlling yobbish behaviour emerged as the top priority – cited by 37% of those surveyed – followed by increased security camera surveillance (21%).

Commenting on the results, Simon Clark, director of FOREST, said: 'The research confirms that the British public do not support a complete ban on smoking in public places. They want more smoke-free areas and well-ventilated pubs, and they prefer choice rather than an outright ban.

'Smoking isn't a crime and it is important that politicians recognise that smokers need somewhere where they can smoke in comfort without being ostracised from their non-smoking friends, the majority of whom want restrictions, not a total ban.'

Explaining why FOREST has taken the unusual step of advertising the poll results, Clark said: 'Members of the public who don't want a ban, whether they are smokers or non-smokers, shouldn't be complacent that it won't happen here. That's why we're fighting for choice. People should make their views known now to local councillors and MPs as well as taking an active part in local consultation.'

*'The research confirms that the British public do not support a complete ban on smoking in public places. They want more smoke-free areas and well-ventilated pubs, and they prefer choice rather than an outright ban.'*

Simon Clark, Director, FOREST, 25 May 2004

## Main points:

■ Seven out of ten (74%) people do not support a ban on smoking in pubs, clubs and bars.

■ Most (68%) think there should be separate smoking and non-smoking areas, with the majority favouring mainly non-smoking with separate smoking areas.

■ Only 24% of people think smoking should be banned completely in all pubs, bars and clubs.

■ 63% agree that decisions on smoking policy should be left to owners and managers of pubs, clubs and bars, rather than local or central government.

■ The majority (56%), including the same proportion of smokers and non-smokers, agree that pub environments have significantly improved and are noticeably less smoky.

■ Two-thirds (66%) agree that the number of non-smoking areas/venues has increased, though 80% say that improvements are still required.

■ Of those not in favour of a ban (74%), the vast proportion (93%) say it's better to have a choice of smoking or non-smoking facilities than banning it altogether.

*Notes:*

1. The research was carried out by Populus by way of a random telephone poll of 10,000 adults aged 18+ and living in Great Britain, between 20 April and 2 May 2004.

2. 1,000 interviews were conducted in each of eight cities – Birmingham, Brighton, Bristol, Cardiff, Leeds, Liverpool, Greater Manchester and Sheffield – and in the North East region of England, and Scotland.

3. Executive Summary and Statistical Data on the findings available upon request. Full report available on the FOREST website from Tuesday 25 May 2004.

■ The above information is from FOREST's website which can be found at www.forestonline.org

© FOREST

# Smoking in public places

## An independent survey of public attitudes to smoking in pubs, bars and clubs

### Banning smoking is not high on community priorities

| Which of the following do you think should be your local council's HIGHEST priority to improve quality of life locally? | ALL 10,000 |
|---|---|
| Controlling yobbish behaviour | 37% |
| Increased security camera surveillance | 21% |
| Banning smoking in public places | 15% |
| Maintaining parks and open spaces | 10% |
| Prohibiting litter and graffiti | 9% |
| Banning cars in city centre | 5% |
| Other | 1% |
| Don't know | 1% |
| None of these | 1% |

### General attitudes to smoking in pubs, clubs and bars

| Thinking only about smoking in pubs, bars and clubs, which of the following BEST describes your view? | ALL 10,000 |
|---|---|
| Smoking should be allowed in venues with good ventilation and non-smoking areas | 28% |
| I would like smoking banned altogether | 22% |
| Provided there is a real choice of smoking and non-smoking facilities, I am happy | 19% |
| The smoking situation doesn't really bother me | 12% |
| Smoking should not be allowed at the bar in the interests of staff | 10% |
| I would like to see more non-smoking facilities | 9% |
| Don't know | 1% |

*Source: FOREST*

### How should smoking be dealt with in pubs, clubs and bars?

| Which of the following statements is closest to your view about the way smoking should be dealt with in pubs, clubs and bars? | ALL 10,000 |
|---|---|
| Smoking should be allowed throughout all pubs, clubs and bars | 6% |
| All pubs, bars and clubs should be mainly smoking with separate non-smoking areas | 19% |
| All pubs, bars and clubs should be mainly non-smoking with separate areas for smoking | 49% |
| Smoking should be banned completely in all pubs, bars and clubs | 24% |
| Don't know | 1% |

### Reasons for not supporting a ban on smoking in pubs, bars and clubs

| I am going to read out some reasons some people have given for not supporting a ban on smoking in pubs, bars and clubs. Please say in each case if you agree or disagree. | ALL 10,000 |
|---|---|
| It's better to have a choice of smoking or non-smoking facilities than banning it altogether | 93% |
| A ban would harm the business prospects of pubs, clubs and bars | 77% |
| A ban infringes people's rights | 76% |
| Smoking is part of the atmosphere of pubs, clubs and bars | 73% |
| Smoking doesn't bother me | 71% |
| It would be divisive because you couldn't socialise with smokers | 62% |

# Is this the end of smoking in public?

## A total ban on smoking could be introduced by 2007

**By Matthew Hickey**

A nationwide ban on smoking in all pubs and restaurants could be on its way. The Government has rejected voluntary restrictions and plans a legal crackdown.

The success of similar bans in Ireland, California and New York City is believed to be behind the move.

However, to avoid a backlash from 13 million smokers, the Government could hand responsibility for imposing the ban to local authorities – a move scorned by leisure industry chiefs yesterday.

While they acknowledge that public opinion is swinging behind the idea of smoke-free pubs and bars, they say the ban must be total.

Smoke-free zones imposed by local authorities would lead to chaos, they warn, with smoking in pubs on one side of the street and a ban on the other.

Following bans in the US and Ireland, similar laws are also on the way in Holland, Norway and Sweden.

### Improving public health

In Britain, ministers are determined to cut the number of smokers – currently stable at one adult in four – in order to meet targets on improving public health.

But they believe that in curbing tobacco advertising, raising tax on cigarettes and putting larger warnings on packets they have gone as far as they can without tightening the law on where smokers can light up.

At the same time, growing evidence of the dangers from passive smoking has left pubs and restaurants facing a time bomb of compensation claims from staff forced to work in smoky rooms.

Culture Secretary Tessa Jowell and Health Minister Melanie Johnson held a meeting last week with the British Hospitality Association to hear the industry's latest ideas for a tougher voluntary code of conduct, which they hope will prevent a legal ban from harming their trade.

They included banning smoking while actually standing at the bar in pubs by 2006, and introducing no smoking areas to 80 per cent of pubs by 2007.

### Public places

Ministers made it clear that this did not go far enough, and the proposals have effectively been sidelined.

Instead, Labour is consulting on a plan to let local authorities ban smoking in public places as part of the party's Big Conversation – a nationwide series of debates ahead of the General Election, which is likely to be next year.

Several major cities are lining up to use such powers, including Manchester and Liverpool – which wants to bring in a ban by 2008 when it becomes European City of Culture.

The Department of Health is also looking at the issue as part of a drive to cut the 120,000 deaths caused by smoking-related illness.

Bob Cotton, chief executive of the British Hospitality Association, who attended last week's meeting, said: 'If the feedback from Labour's Big Conversation leans strongly towards a ban, then I think we'll see it as a manifesto pledge.

'If it's less clear, I think they will stick with a voluntary code for two or three more years, while waiting for public opinion to harden up.'

### Compensation threat

The pressure group Action on Smoking and Health (ASH) claims change is inevitable, because of the threat of compensation lawsuits by bar staff.

A spokesman said: 'The key legal point is the date when employers can be judged to have "guilty knowledge", knowing that a system of work is dangerous, such as exposing bar staff to passive smoking.

'A vast majority of experts now say passive smoking is dangerous, so anybody being made ill at this moment from passive smoking in the workplace will have a claim for compensation.'

■ This article first appeared in the *Daily Mail*, 10 May 2004.

# Want out of smoking?

## Information from No Smoking Day

### Want out of illness?

Smoking has more than 50 ways of making you sick through illness and more than 20 ways of killing you. In general, smokers endure poorer health than non-smokers. People who Want out of Smoking account for 8 million consultations with GPs and over 7 million prescriptions each year.

### Non-lethal illness

Smokers face a higher risk than non-smokers for a wide variety of illnesses, many of which may be fatal (see 'Deaths caused by smoking' below).

### Increased risk of sickness for smokers

- Acute necrotising ulcerative gingivitis (gum disease)
- Angina (20x risk)
- Back pain
- Buerger's Disease (severe circulatory disease)
- Cataract (2x risk)
- Cataract, posterior subcapsular (3x risk)
- Colon Polyps
- Crohn's Disease (chronic inflamed bowel)
- Depression
- Duodenal ulcer
- Diabetes (Type 2, non-insulin dependent)
- Hearing loss
- Influenza
- Impotence (2x risk)
- Ligament injuries
- Macular degeneration (eyes, 2x risk)
- Muscle injuries
- Neck pain
- Nystagmus (abnormal eye movements)
- Ocular Histoplasmosis (fungal eye infection)
- Optic Neuropathy (loss of vision, 16x risk)
- Osteoporosis (in both sexes)
- Osteoarthritis
- Penis (inability to have an erection)
- Peripheral vascular disease
- Pneumonia
- Psoriasis (2x risk)
- Skin wrinkling (2x risk)
- Stomach ulcer
- Rheumatoid arthritis (for heavy smokers)
- Tendon injuries
- Tobacco Amblyopia (loss of vision)
- Tooth loss
- Tuberculosis

### Function impaired in smokers

- Ejaculation (volume reduced)
- Fertility (30% lower in women)
- Immune System (impaired)
- Menopause (onset 1.74 years nearly on average)
- Sperm count reduced
- Sperm motility impaired
- Sperm less able to penetrate the ovum
- Sperm shape abnormalities increased

### Symptoms worse in smokers

- Asthma
- Chronic rhinitis (chronic inflammation of the nose)
- Diabetic retinopathy (eyes)
- Graves' disease (over-active thyroid gland)
- Multiple Sclerosis
- Optic Neuritis (eyes)

### Disease more severe or persistent in smokers

- Common cold
- Crohn's Disease (chronic inflamed bowel)
- Influenza
- Pneumonia
- Tuberculosis

Deaths caused by smoking are six times higher than deaths arising from: road accidents (3,444); poisoning and overdose (2,663); other accidental deaths (8,986); murder and manslaughter (503); suicide (4,379); and HIV infection (195) added together!

### Passive smoking

Passive smoking causes death and disease.

Second-hand smoke is the main cause of indoor air pollution. At least one thousand people are estimated to die each year in the UK as the result of exposure to other people's tobacco smoke.

Exposure to second-hand smoke increases the risk of lung cancer by 20-30% and the risk of coronary heart disease by 25-35%.

Passive smoking increases the risk of stroke by 80% in non-smoking partners of smokers.

### Passive smoking and children

Children are at particular risk from passive smoking. In the UK today approximately 42% of children and 21% of non-smoking adults live in a household where at least one person smokes.

Exposure to second-hand smoke during pregnancy is linked to low birth weight. The greater the exposure, the greater the risk of a low birth weight baby. Passive smoking has also been found to increase the risk of giving birth prematurely and to leukaemia-associated genetic alterations in the foetus.

Passive smoking is a cause of cot death (sudden infant death syndrome or SIDS).

Each year over 17,000 children under the age of five are admitted to hospital because of the effects of passive smoking.

Children exposed to smoking at home are twice as likely to suffer from asthma or bronchitis and have a far higher absence rate from school as a result of illness.

Children of smoking parents are three times as likely to become smokers.

### Passive smoking and the workplace

The economic costs of passive smoking in the workplace are considerable. They include increased levels of absenteeism through illness and reduced productivity.

Exposure to second-hand smoke in the workplace is linked to work disability caused by respiratory conditions, especially adult asthma.

## Want out of sexual problems?

Women who smoke may have decreased fertility. Smokers are 3 times more likely than non-smokers to take more than one year to conceive.

The quality of sperm in men who smoke is less than non-smokers. Its density is decreased, individual sperm are more likely to be deformed and they find it harder to penetrate the woman's egg.

120,000 men in the UK are impotent as a consequence of smoking. 40% of impotent men are smokers compared to 28% of the general population.

## Sick of smoking and pregnancy

Almost one-third of pregnant women in the UK smoke.

For younger women, smoking and the use of oral contraceptives increases the risk of a heart attack, stroke or other cardiovascular disease tenfold.

Babies born to women who smoke are on average 200 grams (8ozs) lighter than babies born to non-smoking mothers.

The risk of miscarriage is substantially higher in women who smoke.

365 cot deaths a year in England and Wales are attributable to the mother smoking during pregnancy.

## Want out of spending?

A 20-a-day smoker spends approximately £1,600 on cigarettes a year.

The cost of smoking-related absenteeism to industry in the UK is approximately £3 billion.

The cost to the NHS of treating diseases causes by smoking is approximately £1.5 billion a year. This excludes the costs of paying benefits to those suffering from smoking-related disease and the dependants of those who die as a result of smoking.

The Treasury earned £9,510 million in revenue from tobacco tax for the financial year 2000-2001.

The price of a pack of 20 premium brand cigarettes is currently £4.40 of which £3.51 is tax.

Imperial Tobacco and Gallaher control about 80% of the UK market.

In 2001 they reported operating profits of £604 million and £446 million respectively.

## Want out of smoking-related fire?

Discarded smokers' materials cause 9% of house fires.

Smoking causes 12% of accidental fires in the workplace.

41% of house fire deaths (132) in 1999 were from fires started by smoking-related materials. Smoking-related materials were the most frequent cause of house fire resulting in death.

## Want out of looking bad?

Smokers have 2-3 times more chance of developing psoriasis, a chronic skin condition that can be extremely uncomfortable and disfiguring.

The more a person smokes the more likely they are to experience premature wrinkling. Smokers in their 40s often have as many facial wrinkles as a non-smoker in their 60s.

Puckering the mouth and sucking in the cheeks can also cause a long-time smoker to appear gaunt, with wrinkled lips.

Smokers are more likely to store fat around the waist and upper torso than the hips.

The average weight gain when stopping smoking is approximately 2-3 kilos.

■ The above information is from No Smoking Day's website which can be found at www.nosmokingday.org.uk

*© No Smoking Day*

HERE LIES
CONSTANCE
SMOH-KERR

"CAN ANYONE
SPARE
A FAG ?"

# Smoking

## Information from the National Youth Agency (NYA)

Tobacco is a very dangerous drug. It is legal and widely used. Thousands and thousands of people die every year as a result of smoking cigarettes, cigars and pipes. The combined effects of nicotine (the main drug in tobacco), and other gases which enter the lungs when smoked, greatly increase the chance of disease and ill-health. Tobacco is a stimulant drug giving smokers a 'lift'.

Smoking has been directly linked to lung cancer, heart disease and other major illnesses, as well as being dangerous during pregnancy for the mother and unborn child.

It is also recognised that secondary smoking or passive smoking can put the health of others at risk. This is one of the reasons why smoking has been so widely banned in public places.

### Smoking and young people

Although the number of adults who smoke has dropped over the past ten years, this has not happened amongst young people. In fact in some parts of the country the number of young smokers has actually increased especially amongst young women.

Statistics have shown that one-quarter of Britain's 15-year-olds (both boys and girls) are regular smokers. It is estimated that 450 children per day start smoking. Half of all teenagers who are currently smoking will die from diseases caused by tobacco if they continue to smoke throughout their lives and one-half of this number will have their lives shortened by an average of 23 years.

Currently one in five 15-year-old boys smoke cigarettes – this is a decrease of 5% since the mid 1980s. The numbers of teenage girls smoking has risen from 25% in the mid 1980s to 29% now – that's one in three.

### Giving up smoking

Giving up smoking can be very difficult. To follow is some information about using nicotine patches or gum to help.

### Nicotine patches

There are a number of nicotine skin patches on the market. Take a look in the chemist or supermarket. The patch looks like a sticking plaster and is applied to dry non-hairy skin, for example on the upper arm. A patch lasts for between 16 and 24 hours and they come in three different strengths delivering different amounts of nicotine directly through the skin. You are recommended to use them for between 8 and 12 weeks. The patches are very easy to use and work by slowly building up your nicotine level throughout the day. This reduces your cravings and although you may still get the urge to have a cigarette, your thoughts about smoking will not be as strong as they were before.

Research has shown that using patches can double your chances of giving up smoking. They are most helpful to people who have been moderate smokers (10-20 cigarettes a day). The problem with using patches is they don't provide you with an alternative 'activity' to help with the physical withdrawal symptoms. Many smokers fail to give up because they enjoy the actual 'action' of smoking, lighting the cigarette and holding it.

### Nicotine gum

The gum option has been equally successful and does give smokers something to actually 'do'. The gum is different from normal chewing gum and has a peppery flavour that tingles on your tongue – something you may take time getting used to! The recommended amount is one piece per hour. The gum is available in two strengths and works by slowly releasing nicotine that is absorbed through the lining of your mouth. It is suggested that you use the gum for up to 3 months.

Some ex-smokers have reported being unable to give up the gum even though they have successfully quit the cigarettes! The good news is that this seems to lessen with time and remember, the gum is far safer than smoking cigarettes.

### Smoking and advertising

The Tobacco Advertising and Promotion Act came into effect on 14 February 2003. The Act outlaws adverts for cigarettes in magazines, newspapers, on the internet and on billboards. Sponsorship of Formula 1 racing and other 'global sporting events' will continue until 2006 at the latest. The British Medical Association has also called for smoking to be banned in public places.

■ The above information is from www.youthinformation.com by the National Youth Agency

© National Youth Agency (NYA)

# The QUIT guide to teen quitting

If you're a teenage smoker, you know that smoking kills. You know that it causes cancer and heart disease, strokes and emphysema. That it reduces female fertility and induces male impotence. That it destroys your fitness, wrecks your skin and drains your bank balance.

There's nothing worse than being told, over and over, not to smoke. That smoking's bad for you, that you're too young.

Smoking is a matter of choice. If you want to smoke, you smoke. But it pays to make an informed choice and to step back sometimes – to ask yourself, 'Do I really want to smoke?' If you have doubts, think. Why do you smoke? What do you know about smoking? And about quitting? Where can you find out more?

It's a big issue, and a massive decision. It pays to be informed. A good first source of information is the internet. If you have access, log on to www.ash.org.uk for smoking facts and www.quit.org.uk for quitting tips. Both these sites have excellent links to sites covering all aspects of the habit. You've found the facts. Maybe you want to smoke. Maybe you want to quit. If you want to pack it in, now what?

First, make sure you really want to pack it in. It's easy enough to make that spur-of-the-moment decision; to go for a few hours, even a day or two without a cigarette, then to feel tempted; 'one won't hurt', then another one, a few more: oops you're back where you started. To stand any chance at all of success, you have to be absolutely determined to quit; you have to know why you want to quit and how you're going to do it.

Quitting can be hard. Very hard. You probably feel that you need cigarettes. The majority of smokers are addicts – addicted to the nicotine in cigarettes and reliant on the smoking routine, on smoking be-

**QUIT®**
Helping smokers to quit

haviour and the smoking lifestyle. But don't assume that you're an addict, that you'll find quitting a nightmare. If you're determined to stop, stop. If you experience withdrawal symptoms – if you feel anxious, nauseous, headachy, if you cannot go without a cigarette – you'll need more help.

Quitting 'cold turkey' is quitting the simplest way, just stopping smoking. It's not a nice name. The reality, though, isn't always so grim. Plenty of smokers make the decision to stop, stub out and stay smoke free. It's well worth giving cold turkey a chance. Just be prepared, and focused, and don't mistake a lack of willpower for a lack of support. Services like the freephone Quitline – 0800 00 22 00 – are there to help. Remember, the vast majority of successful quitters quit without touching a cessation product.

That's not to say, though, that cessation products can't make a major difference. Nicotine Replacement Therapy (NRT) and Zyban have both been proven to double a smoker's chances of quitting success-

fully. Both are NHS prescribable. Both courses last around eight weeks. They're enormously effective – a real breakthrough. Great, but how do they work and, crucially, can teenagers use them?

## Products

Zyban, also called bupropion, doesn't contain nicotine. Technically a 'dopamine reuptake inhibitor', it stops you feeling the dopamine rush that nicotine unlocks when you inhale and dampens cravings and withdrawal. Zyban hasn't been extensively tested on under-18s. Because of this, and because it's associated with a small incidence of dangerous side effects in adults, Zyban, a prescription-only drug, is not recommended for, or licensed for use by, people aged under 18. Further studies are needed. If you're 18 or over, and interested in Zyban, speak to your GP.

NRT employs Nicotine Replacement Products (NRPs) to give you a small, safe dose of nicotine. This dose helps you to stop smoking by easing withdrawal symptoms. You cut it down gradually until you're nicotine free. The best-known NRT 'delivery systems' are nicotine patches and gums. Inhalators, lozenges, nasal sprays and sublingual (under the tongue) tablets are other options. NRPs haven't been comprehensively tested on (under-18) teenagers. That's why they're either labelled 'Not for sale to or use by children' or 'Not for use by persons under the age of 18 unless recommended by a doctor.'

So, speak to your doctor. NRT might be an option. Zyban, unless you're 18 or over, won't be. Your GP knows your circumstances and can make the right decision. If he, or she, does prescribe you NRPs, make sure he, or she, or your pharmacist, explains exactly how you should use them.

There's a very good chance, though, that you won't need and/or won't be prescribed any cessation drug. Either way, remember: the most important thing is your attitude. Address the underlying reasons why you smoke and why you want to give up.

The most accessible, the cheapest, and arguably the best, help you'll get comes from talking. Discussing what you're going through can make the whole process much, much easier. Your friends are an obvious choice. They might even smoke, but if they're real friends, they'll want to help. In fact, if they smoke, they're more likely to understand why you want to stop and how hard it is to do. They might just want to stop with you.

## Services

You'll almost certainly want to talk. But friends and family aren't necessarily an option. Teachers, doctors and pharmacists may not be right either. Helplines offer an excellent alternative. Calling the Quitline, for instance, on 0800 00 22 00, puts you in touch with a team of trained counsellors. Don't be put off by the word 'counsellor'. The Quitline team are as ready to offer simple practical advice to suit your circumstances as to lend support and an understanding ear. Counsellors can refer you to a range of resources to help you and provide an absolutely confidential service. Your call is free and won't – if your household uses BT – show up on the phone bill.

QUIT, the charity behind the Quitline, has recently launched a QUIT e-counselling service. You can e-mail QUIT counsellors on stopsmoking@quit.org.uk. They'll get back to you the same day or – if you e-mail late – the next day, with advice, support and/or information. QUIT counsellors are 100% flexible. You might want to call, or e-mail, every day, to discuss how you're getting on and to work through any problems. Or you might want to make one or two quick calls to talk through your options. Totally up to you.

QUIT runs Break Free, a programme designed to help young people decide for themselves: is smoking worth it? You can request a Break Free pack of eight fact-packed postcards by calling the Quitline or e-mailing stopsmoking@quit.org.uk. Break Free works closely with

schools. Break Free presenters give students the facts to make an informed decision. Their presentations are fun – but credible – and very informative.

Break Free also organises confidential, and voluntary, support sessions. For these, a counsellor visits a school once a week for seven weeks, usually at lunchtime, and helps students who want to stop smoking. If you'd like your school to organise support sessions, ask a teacher to give the QUIT office a call on 020 7251 1551 for more information. Schools presentations aren't currently available across the country, but, again, if you're interested, ask a teacher to ask.

There's a chance that the 'asking teacher' routine isn't your preferred scenario. A good chance. If that's the case – but you are interested in seeing a Break Free presentation or attending Break Free support sessions – e-mail us the name of your school, or phone the Quitline with the details. We'll make contact and explain what we can offer. We won't mention your name or your call.

QUIT's services aren't your only avenue of support. For information on other free services, which could include NHS smoking clinics and schemes tailored to your region, you should call the Quitline, e-mail stopsmoking@quit.org.uk, search the net, and/or look out for leaflets in your school/local library/health centre. You could ask a 'responsible adult'.

## QUIT tips

There's plenty of help out there. But if you want to go it alone, that's fine. Just make a plan and stick to it. Here are some tips.

Set a quit date. Decide when you want to quit. You might want to stop smoking at a special time; on New Year's Day, or on No Smoking Day. You could stop as a (fantastic) birthday present for someone special.

Keep a smoking diary for a week or two before your quit date. Write

down when and where you smoke – or want to smoke. Whether you enjoy each cigarette. How you feel. This'll give you an idea of what to watch out for – where you might want to change your routine. If you always smoke after your evening meal, for instance, give yourself an alternative. Suck a sweet or a lollipop. Read a magazine. If you like computer games, play one.

Get rid of your cigarettes. All of them. If you're keeping a few aside 'in case', or if you're 'hiding them' (from yourself?), you need to think very hard about whether you do actually want to quit. The best idea is to pour water into the pack(s) before you bin it/them. That way, you won't be tempted to rummage for a sneaky smoke. You should also get rid of your lighter(s), matches and any ashtrays.

Keep ultra busy, and stock up on treats to distract you if and when your mind starts wandering where it shouldn't. You might want to buy a CD or two that you know you'll want to listen to. Or a DVD to watch. Maybe a game for your console. Even a console. OK, these are expensive options, but a lot less expensive than your year's supply of cigarettes.

Don't worry about your weight. You may put on a pound or two when you quit. If you do, it's because you feel hungry and you're eating more. That's fine. Snacking can be an excellent way to keep your mind off cravings and can be a big help in beating the baccy. Accept that your diet may go downhill for a few weeks. When you're a happy, healthy non-smoker, a few weeks in, just use a dash of the willpower you used to quit smoking to cut the calories. Easy.

As time goes on, think about how well you've done. Are you going to throw it away for a quick drag? Remember, nicotine addiction can be conquered fairly quickly. If you're still missing cigarettes after a few weeks, you're just missing a memory. Remind yourself why you wanted to quit. Read a page or two of your smoking diary. Then congratulate yourself: you're a healthy non-smoker, not dependent on anything. Should feel pretty good. If you're vain, take a look in the mirror at that smoke-free hunk or honey.

© QUIT

# Stopping smoking

## ASH's 15 tips

### 1. Get professional help . . .

Ring the helpline on Freephone 0800 169 0 169 for information and advice. Pregnant women seeking help in stopping smoking can call the pregnancy Quitline on 0800 169 9169. Specialist helplines are also available in Asian languages. Your doctor, pharmacist, or health visitor should also give advice and they should tell you if there are special services for smokers in your area. See also ASH's quitting links for further help and resources.

### 2. Prepare mentally . . .

You are not alone! 70% of British smokers would like to quit and about three million try each year. More than 11 million people in Britain have quit and are now ex-smokers. However, it can be tough and you will need lots of willpower to break the hold of nicotine – a powerful and addictive drug. An important part of this is to know what you would gain and what you would lose from stopping smoking. One ex-60-a-day smoker (Allen Carr, author of best-selling *The Easy Way to Stop Smoking*) says: 'there is absolutely nothing to give up . . . there is no genuine pleasure or crutch in smoking. It is just an illusion, like banging your head against a wall to make it pleasant when you stop.'

### 3. Demolish smoking myths . . .

Soon after smoking a cigarette the body and brain start to want more nicotine and many people begin to feel increasingly uncomfortable until they have the next cigarette. Smoking feels pleasurable, but much of the pleasure of smoking is relief of withdrawal from nicotine. There are times that many people feel distracted or unable to enjoy themselves because they were not able to smoke. This is nicotine withdrawal in action. If you see it this way, cigarettes are not a familiar friend but more like a greedy parasite demanding constant attention.

## ash.
### action on smoking and health

### 4. Understand what to expect . . .

Most people find the first few days difficult and for some it can be a long struggle, but things will typically start to get better after the third or fourth day. Nicotine withdrawal may make you restless, irritable, frustrated, sleepless, or accident prone – but these things will pass and you will quickly start to feel the benefits. See the ASH fact sheet on what happens when you give up smoking.

### 5. Make a list of reasons why you want to stop smoking . . .

It means different things to different people, but if you know what you want from stopping, it could help you through the most difficult moments. Reasons could include some or all of:

- Better all-round health – stopping smoking reduces risk of 50 different illnesses and conditions
- Heart attack risk drops to the same as a non-smoker three years after quitting
- Cancer risk drops with every year of not smoking
- Live longer and stay well – one in two long-term smokers die early and lose about 16 years of life
- Set a good example to the kids (or other people's kids) – don't want to be a smoking role model
- Have lots of money to spend on other things – smoking 20 a day can cost £1,600 per year
- Improved fitness and easier breathing – better at sports and getting up stairs
- Better chance of having a healthy baby
- Food and drink tastes better
- Better skin and complexion, and no early wrinkles
- Fresher smelling breath, hair and clothes, and no more cigarette smells around the house
- Back in full control and no longer craving or distracted when I am not smoking or not able to smoke
- Travel on trains, aircraft, buses will be easier
- Work will be easier and I won't have to spend so much time outside or in the smoking room
- Don't want to support tobacco companies
- Concern about environmental impact of tobacco growing
- Other .........................................

## 6. Consider the money . . .

Main brand cigarettes now cost £4.48 after the April 2003 budget. The table shows how much smoking costs at current prices.

| | Years of smoking | | | | |
| Cigarettes per day | 1 | 5 | 10 | 20 | 50 |
|---|---|---|---|---|---|
| 5 | £409 | £2,044 | £4,088 | £8,176 | £20,440 |
| 10 | £818 | £4,088 | £8,176 | £16,352 | £40,880 |
| 20 | £1,635 | £8,176 | £16,352 | £32,704 | £81,760 |
| 40 | £3,270 | £16,352 | £32,704 | £65,408 | £163,520 |

### 7. Set a date . . .

Some people make a New Year's Day resolution, others pick their birthday, and you can join in with others on No Smoking Day – the second Wednesday of every March – when up to a million smokers have a go. Any day will do, but choosing a date will help mental preparation.

### 8. Involve friends or family . . .

If you live with someone else that smokes, it will be much easier to quit if you do it together. When expecting a baby, both parents should do it together. One common mistake is not to take the effort to quit smoking seriously enough. Really putting your whole commitment behind it will help you have the right frame of mind to face the challenge.

### 9. Deal with nicotine withdrawal . . .

Nicotine is a powerful addictive drug (see ASH fact sheet on nicotine) and you can roughly double the chances of successfully quitting smoking by using nicotine replacement therapies such as patches, lozenges, inhalers, and/or gum. The idea is to come off nicotine gradually by using a low nicotine dose to take the edge off the cravings and have a 'soft landing'. Nicotine products include Nicorette, NiQuitin CQ and Nicotinell. An alternative to nicotine products is the drug Zyban which is only available on prescription. Although it is proven to be effective, as with all drugs there is a risk of side effects and you will need to discuss with your doctor whether this form of therapy would be suitable for you.

### 10. Other treatments may help . . .

Hypnosis, acupuncture or other treatments may help some people, but there isn't much formal evidence supporting their effectiveness. Our advice is to use with caution, but even if they help mental preparation, then they have some value. Herbal cigarettes are pointless – you get all the tar, but nothing to help you deal with nicotine withdrawal. Quit has a good guide to treatments.

### 11. Find a (temporary) substitute habit . . .

Smoking also involves having something to do with the hands or mouth. Non-smokers manage without this, so it will not be necessary in the long term. But if this is part of the smoking habit, you may need to deal with it. It might be an idea to use chewing gum, drink more water, fruit juice or tea, or to chew or eat something (but see weight gain below!).

### 12. Deal with any weight-gain worries . . .

Yes, it is true: many people do gain weight when they quit smoking. Nicotine changes the appetite and body's energy use (metabolism). Even if you do gain weight it will be worth it if you quit, but if you want to avoid weight-gain then you can prepare. For example, you can change your diet or avoid alcohol, or take more exercise. (You may find QUIT's guide *Quit smoking without putting on weight* helpful.)

### 13. Avoid temptation . . .

In the difficult first few days you can change your routine to avoid situations where you would usually smoke. For example, it might be worth avoiding the pub on the first Friday night after you quit.

### 14. Stop completely . . .

Although it might seem like a good idea to cut down and then stop, this is actually very difficult to do in practice. If you cut down, the likely response is that you will smoke each cigarette more intensively and end up doing yourself just as much harm. The best approach is to go for a complete break and use nicotine replacement products (see above) to help take the edge off the withdrawal symptoms.

### 15. Watch out for relapse . . .

You will need to be on your guard especially in the first few days and weeks. 'I'll have just one, it can't harm' is the top of a long and slippery slope. If you are upset or under pressure, it is really important to fight off the temptation to smoke – don't let this be an excuse for slipping back. You could lose everything you've achieved just in a momentary lapse.

■ The above information is from Action on Smoking and Health – ASH's website which can be found at www.ash.org.uk

© *Action on Smoking and Health – ASH*

# How smoking habit will cut 10 years off your life

## Study shows 1 in 4 killed by tobacco is middle aged

### By Tim Utton,
### Science Reporter

Smokers die ten years earlier on average than non-smokers, according to a devastating study of the effects of tobacco.

Findings published 22 June 2004 of the 50-year survey show that up to two-thirds of life-long cigarette smokers are killed by their habit.

Of those, at least one in four will die in middle age from smoking-related diseases including cancer, stroke and heart disease.

The study – the biggest-ever into tobacco – was led by Oxford professor Sir Richard Doll, who first discovered the link between tobacco and cancer.

It concludes that the early deaths of smokers mean a British man who smoked from his teens could expect to live only to 66.

In addition, his later years are likely to be blighted by smoking-related ill health.

The research is being hailed as the most accurate indicator yet of the hazards faced by the 24 per cent of Britons who still smoke today.

It was started in 1951 by Professor Doll, who is now 91. The results are being published by the *British Medical Journal*.

Prof Doll has tracked 34,000 British doctors since the early 1950s, when he published his ground-breaking work showing a link between smoking and cancer. Only 134 of his subjects were alive in 2001. In the half century since he started his study, tobacco has killed about six million people in Britain and 60 million across the developed world.

The professor himself stopped smoking at 37 and his own life reflects another key finding in his study, that the damage caused by tobacco is not irreparable.

Smokers who stop by the age of 50 halve their risk of dying prematurely from a smoking-related disease while those who quit at 30 avoid almost all the risks.

The findings come as the debate on a public smoking ban continues, with Tony Blair signalling in early June 2004 that the habit could soon be barred in pubs, restaurants and the workplace.

### The early deaths of smokers mean a British man who smoked from his teens could expect to live only to 66

Because of Professor Doll's stature in the medical world, his study is likely to have a significant influence on health officials. Ian Willmore, spokesman for the anti-smoking group Action on Smoking and Health, said: 'This research shows just how much damage is being done by smoking.

'If you smoke, it basically wipes out all the advances of medical science of the last 50 years, in terms of life expectancy. We think the next step is to end smoking in the workplace.'

Meanwhile, research at Boston University School of Medicine suggests that smokers could be screened to identify those at risk of lung cancer.

Scientists have found that smokers who contract lung cancer may have genes that give only poor protection against tumours forming in the lungs.

Although cigarette smoking is responsible for 90 per cent of all lung cancers, only 10 per cent to 15 per cent of people who smoke end up with the disease.

The study is reported in *Proceedings of the National Academy of Science*.

In another report, the US Surgeon General, Richard Carmona said that every organ in the body is harmed by cigarettes.

He detailed dozens of diseases that are now linked to tobacco use including cancer of the stomach, cervix, pancreas and kidney. Pneumonia, various types of leukaemia, gum diseases and even cataracts are also related to the habit. And a further study from Ohio State University suggests that smokers who cut down instead of giving up completely are fooling themselves.

This is because they quickly change the way they smoke to make up for cutting down.

Those who smoked 50 per cent fewer cigarettes took larger and more frequent puffs and smoked more of a cigarette before stubbing it out.

This left them more vulnerable to cancer-causing chemicals.

© *The Daily Mail, June 2004*

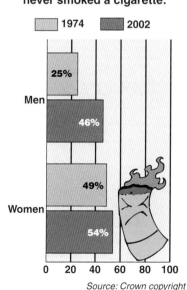

**Never smoked**

There has been an increase in the proportion of men and women aged 16 and over who have never smoked a cigarette.

1974    2002

Men  25%  46%

Women  49%  54%

0  20  40  60  80  100

*Source: Crown copyright*

# Low tar exposed

## The truth

*'Low tar' cigarettes aren't as dangerous as regular ones . . . are they?*
Unfortunately they are.

Research shows that smokers of 'light' or 'mild' brands are likely to inhale as much tar and nicotine as smokers of regular cigarettes. This means they can take in as many cancer-causing poisons as smokers of regular cigarettes.

In simple terms, 'low tar' cigarettes are just as harmful as regular cigarettes.

### Tar readings

*I thought 'light' cigarettes had lower tar readings?*
You might think the tar and nicotine quantities displayed on the side of cigarette packs would correspond to the levels you actually breathe in – but they don't!

These measurements are confusing as they don't tell you what you need to know. They come from tests performed by a machine and not from tests with real people.

The readings produced by the machine do not reflect the amount of tar and nicotine that a real person inhales if they smoke 'low tar' cigarettes.

*Why don't the readings represent what smokers actually breathe in?*
- The testing machine has a mechanical mouth that 'smokes' a cigarette to analyse its contents.
- To test the amount of tar and nicotine yielded by a cigarette, the machine 'inhales' one 35ml puff lasting 2 seconds, every minute until the cigarette burns down to a certain length.
- The amounts of tar and nicotine drawn into the machine are then measured. These are the measurements that appear on the side of packs.
- But real people do not smoke 'low tar' cigarettes the same way as the testing machine.

CANCER RESEARCH UK

- Real people smoke a 'low tar' cigarette much more intensively than the test machine and therefore inhale a greater quantity of tar and nicotine than is recorded in machine tests.
- The same effect occurs in relation to tar. Tar intake is higher than shown on the pack.

### The taste

*Why do 'low tar' cigarettes taste weaker?*
Tiny holes in the filters of 'low tar' cigarettes cause air to mix with the smoke, which is inhaled by 'low tar' smokers.

This makes the smoke from 'low tar' cigarettes taste weaker or less harsh than smoke from regular cigarettes.

*How do 'low tar' smokers end up inhaling just as much tar?*
- Research shows that the dilution effect caused by filter holes leads many smokers of 'low tar' brands to smoke more intensively than if they smoked regular cigarettes.
- People smoke in this way, often without even realising, in order to inhale enough nicotine from their 'low tar' cigarettes to get a satisfying smoke.

---

*Research shows that smokers of 'light' or 'mild' brands are likely to inhale as much tar and nicotine as smokers of regular cigarettes*

---

- Also, in many cases, the dilution effect caused by filter holes is reduced because many smokers of 'low tar' cigarettes accidentally block the holes with their fingers or lips.

*So, the weaker taste of 'light' cigarettes can be deceptive?*
That's right. Because of the way people smoke 'light' cigarettes, they can end up inhaling as much tar and nicotine as if they smoked regular cigarettes.

### How people smoke 'lights'

Research shows that smokers of 'light' cigarettes:
- inhale more smoke from their cigarette
- take more puffs from their cigarette
- smoke a greater proportion of each cigarette
- cover up the small holes in the filters on their cigarette, increasing the strength of the smoke they breathe in.

People who smoke 'low tar' cigarettes will often do some or all of these things without even realising it.

This is because they are subconsciously trying to inhale enough nicotine from their 'low tar' cigarette for a more satisfying smoke.

*So 'low tar' cigarettes aren't actually 'low tar' at all?*
- No they're not. Supposedly 'low tar' cigarettes can deliver as much tar and other cancer-causing poisons to your lungs as regular brands.
- All smokers are at risk of developing smoking-related diseases such as cancer, heart disease, stroke and emphysema.

- The above information is from Cancer Research UK's Light & Mild Campaign website which can be found at www.lowtarexposed.org.uk
© *Cancer Research UK*

# Thinking about giving up?

## You can do it!

People who prepare to give up smoking are always the most successful. With its information, practical tips and advice, this guide will help you understand more about why you smoke and the steps you can take to 'give up for life'.

The guide mostly talks about cigarettes, but the same advice applies whether you're giving up smoking cigars or a pipe, or chewing tobacco. 'Cigarettes' include roll-ups as well as manufactured cigarettes.

### Ten top tips

- Contact your local NHS Stop Smoking Service for practical help and advice from trained specialists.
- Plan ahead to help you cope with stressful situations.
- Pick a quit date that will be stress-free, and stick to it.
- Take it one day at a time, and congratulate yourself every day.
- Pair up with someone else who wants to stop so you can support each other.
- Use Nicotine Replacement Therapy (NRT) or bupropion (Zyban) to help you manage the cravings.
- At first, avoid situations where you might be tempted to smoke.
- Keep track of the money you're saving – and treat yourself!
- There's no such thing as having 'just one' cigarette.
- Think positive – you CAN do it!

Now read on for more ideas on giving up for life . . .

### The health benefits of giving up – time stopped and benefits

**20 minutes**
Blood pressure and pulse return to normal.

Circulation improves, especially to hands and feet.

**8 hours**
Blood oxygen levels increase to normal, and your chances of having a heart attack start to fall.

**24 hours**
Carbon monoxide leaves the body.

The lungs start to clear out mucus and debris.

**48 hours**
Your body is now nicotine-free. Your senses of taste and smell begin to improve.

**72 hours**
Breathing is easier, and your energy levels increase.

**2-12 weeks**
Circulation improves throughout the body. Walking and exercise get easier.

**3-9 months**
Breathing problems, coughing, shortness of breath and wheezing improve. Lung efficiency increased by 5-10 per cent.

**5 years**
Risk of having a heart attack falls to about half that of a smoker.

**10 years**
Risk of lung cancer falls to around half that of a smoker.

Risk of a heart attack falls to about the same as someone who has never smoked.

Stopping smoking at any age increases your life expectancy, provided you stop before you develop cancer or other serious disease. But even if damage has already been done, you can still benefit from stopping.

### The cycle of stopping

**Stage 1**
Thinking about stopping.

**Stage 2**
Preparing to stop: proper planning makes you much more likely to succeed.

**Stage 3**
Stopping: set a quit date and stick to it.

**Stage 4**
Staying stopped: changing your attitude to smoking and your lifestyle.

**Stage 5**
Relapsing: this can happen if you weren't really ready to stop, or stopping smoking wasn't what you expected it to be. You haven't failed, so don't feel guilty. Each time you try, even if you don't succeed, you learn valuable lessons that can help you next time.

- The above information is from *Giving up for Life* by the Department of Health.

© *Crown copyright*

## Working out the cost of smoking

Cigarettes don't just damage your health, they're bad news for your bank balance too. Use this space to work out exactly how much you spend on your habit – you might be in for a nasty surprise!
I started smoking when I was _____ years old
I have smoked for a total of _____ years of my life
I spend £ _____ each week on tobacco

Multiply the amount you spend each week by 52 to find out how much you're spending on smoking each year
Total: £ _____ a year

If I don't give up smoking now:
In three years' time I will have spent another £ _____
In five years' time I will have spent another £ _____
In ten years' time I will have spent another £ _____

Write down some of the other things you could spend the money on instead. What about some new clothes? A car? Or a holiday for you and your family?

# In the clear

**The truth about stopping smoking written by people who have done it**

## Benefits of stopping smoking

### Jenny – aged 57

The first thing that made me think about stopping smoking was the money I'd save. We really needed another car and it was easy to see that if I stopped smoking we would save over a hundred pounds a month.

It took me a fair few attempts to get there, but with help from my GP I finally stopped. It's amazing how quickly the money piles up – it seemed like no time at all before we were driving around in our new car.

### Sally and Peter – aged 37

To help motivate us we made a pact to save the money that we would normally spend each week on cigarettes to take our daughter, Georgia, to Disneyland in Paris. She was so excited about the trip we knew we couldn't let her down. She even decorated our savings box with Disney stickers.

After a few months we had enough money to pay for a fabulous short break to Paris. Stopping smoking was not easy but it was definitely worth it to see Georgia having the time of her life.

## Smoking and your health

Nearly everyone now accepts that smoking has many health risks including reduced fertility and increased risk of developing heart disease, cancer and osteoporosis.

The good news is that once you stop smoking, you will immediately reap health benefits and this article is full of tips on how to beat your addiction to nicotine in cigarettes.

The benefits of stopping smoking can include:

- Increased energy levels
- Improved taste and smell
- Improved circulation, making walking and running easier
- Fewer coughs, wheezing and breathing problems
- Increased fertility
- Reduced risk of developing osteoporosis

- Your chances of having a heart attack will be halved within one year of stopping smoking
- Your risk of developing lung cancer will be reduced to that of a non-smoker after 5 to 10 years

### Additional benefits for men:

- Reduced risk of becoming impotent. It is estimated that 120,000 UK men in their 30s and 40s are needlessly impotent as a result of smoking

### Additional benefits for women:

- Lighter and shorter periods
- Increased ability to become pregnant by up to a third
- Reduced risk of early menopause
- Less chance of dying from cervical cancer and breast cancer

## Stopping

### Fiona and Darren – aged 35 and 37

Stopping smoking is a major life change, comparable to buying a house or changing jobs, and we found it important to prepare accordingly. The first step is to set a date way in advance so that you have plenty of time to mentally prepare both yourselves and those close to you.

We also found it very important to change our routines and were amazed how certain situations made us crave for nicotine, in particular going to the pub and the few minutes just after eating our evening meal. In fact, I was so unsure that I would be able to resist smoking down at the pub that I avoided it for six weeks by

which time the strongest cravings had subsided, but it didn't keep Darren out of the pub!

However, we couldn't stop eating our evening meal so we had to find a method other than avoiding food. The first few minutes after our evening meal had always been 'our time' and as we never smoked in the house we frequently argued about who got to go outside for a cigarette first. All this changed when we stopped smoking and the first few evenings around the dining table were almost unbearable as we waited for the cravings to pass. We quickly realised that we needed to fill this time and started drinking coffee after dinner and then went straight from the table to load the dishwasher. As well as the bonus of getting Darren to help me tidy up, this kept us busy and stopped the cravings.

You might not have the same things that make you crave nicotine, but we'd recommend that you work them out well in advance so that you can plan to do something else during that time.

Another very important factor in our success was remembering our motivations to stop smoking. I can still remember how devastated I felt the first time I saw my daughter put a pen in her mouth and imitate me smoking a cigarette. It's only natural for a child to be curious about what her mother is doing, but we were desperately worried that her curiosity might turn to experimentation (especially as my first cigarette was taken from my mother's packet).

It was another event involving my daughter that made me realise the strength of my addiction to nicotine and further motivated me to stop smoking. One day when I was out shopping locally, I had little cash on me and was forced to decide between buying cough medicine for my daughter or a packet of cigarettes for myself. I'm ashamed to say that my addiction proved to be even stronger than my maternal instincts and I bought the cigarettes. This one event proved a massive motivator for me and when I was trying to stop smoking, whenever I was tempted to reach for a cigarette, I remembered the disgust I felt for this decision.

## Top tips

Set a date – commit yourself to a stop date well in advance. Women should choose a date during the two weeks after the start of their period to experience less withdrawal symptoms

Seek help – ask your GP for help in stopping smoking since they can prescribe treatments to help you (and if you wish, refer you to a specially trained nurse or other healthcare professional for support and advice)

Clear out – empty your house, office, car and bags of any cigarettes, lighters or ashtrays

Emotion – try to understand why you use cigarettes as an emotional prop in certain situations and choose a new prop, such as an understanding friend or a telephone helpline such as Quitline

Support – try to find somebody to stop smoking at the same time as you, and turn to family, friends and partners for further support

Stress – remember that the ability of cigarettes to provide stress relief is probably an illusion. In fact, smoking causes added stress because not only does it release the stress hormone adrenalin into the body, but smokers are often thinking about their next cigarette. Smokers tend to feel less stressed once they have stopped smoking for a few weeks, and survey results have shown that many ex-smokers don't think that smoking ever helped them relieve stress

Weight – don't diet and stop smoking at the same time. Put concerns about weight gain into perspective against the damage caused by smoking. You can always tackle any weight gain later, once you have beaten the smoking. Remember that one in two smokers will die from smoking-related diseases

Image – take up an aerobic exercise, as evidence shows it may improve long-term success rates and helps improve mood

Control – avoid situations where you would normally smoke until you can control the situation and not suffer from strong cravings

Action – if it helps, use a substitute for cigarettes – for example play with a pen or try eating low calorie snacks like fruit

Keep busy – rather like giving up any relationship, it is important to keep yourself busy, maybe take up a new hobby or spend time with old friends

No thanks, I don't smoke – don't give in because another smoker wants you to smoke with them. It doesn't make you less of a good friend if you refuse their offer of a cigarette. It's not easy, but every cigarette you say 'no' to is a step on the road to success. Keep going – you can get there

## What happens when you stop smoking?

*One hour*
Your blood pressure will start to fall and circulation improves

*One day*
Your lungs will have started cleaning out the mucus and debris associated with smoking and you will be getting more oxygen into your body and brain

*One week*
You will be able to notice a definite improvement in your breathing

*One month*
Your circulation will have dramatically improved

*One year*
Your risk of having a heart attack has at least halved. Your lung function has improved and you may be able to exercise for much longer than before

*Ten years*
Your risk of lung cancer falls to that of a non-smoker

## Withdrawal symptoms
*Nicole – aged 26*
I knew it was going to be hard to stop smoking and to be honest, that was one of the things that kept me from doing it sooner. My GP explained that it takes time for all the nicotine to clear out of my body, which sounded sensible, and helped me to think about the withdrawal symp-toms as positive things – all that badness leaking out.

I struggled with it for what seemed like ages at the time but looking back it was probably only a couple of weeks, and by then I was starting to feel lots of positive things as well – like taste and smell.

## Weight gain
*Lucy – aged 28*
I wasn't surprised to hear that weight gain is women's greatest concern about stopping smoking. When I smoked people would always say that you could put on a lot of weight if you stopped, and that really put me off trying to give up. However, in my mid twenties I began to see how smoking was affecting my health and appearance and although I was very worried about putting on weight, I became desperate to stop smoking before too much damage was done.

Firstly, I discovered that it's unrealistic to think that you will not gain any weight when you stop smoking (although some people don't), but it's only short-term and I'd encourage you not to stop smoking and diet at the same time – it's simply asking too much of your body.

One of the first things you notice when you give up smoking is that you regain your sense of taste. So don't fill your body with unhealthy foods just as it's being cleansed of all the toxins from smoking. Instead make an effort to pick tasty, healthy foods and stick to regular meal times to avoid snacking between meals.

## Withdrawal symptoms
Below we have outlined the main withdrawal symptoms so that you can anticipate and work to overcome them. Generally these symptoms are short lived.
- Light-headedness
- Night-time awakenings
- Poor concentration
- Craving
- Irritability/aggression
- Depression
- Restlessness
- Increased appetite

■ The above information is from *In the Clear*, a booklet produced by SCAPE – Smoking Cessation Action in Primary carE.

*© SCAPE*

# What happens when you stop smoking

## Information from Action on Smoking and Health (ASH)

### The desire to stop smoking

Many smokers continue smoking not through free choice but because they are addicted to the nicotine in cigarettes. A report by the Royal College of Physicians found that nicotine complied with the established criteria for defining an addictive substance. The report states: 'On present evidence, it is reasonable to conclude that nicotine delivered through tobacco smoke should be regarded as an addictive drug, and tobacco use as the means of nicotine self-administration.' [1]

Surveys have consistently shown that at least 70% of adult smokers would like to stop smoking.[2] A 1999 survey found that, of those who expressed a desire to quit, a third were very keen to stop.[2] The same survey found that the more a person smokes the less faith that person has that he or she can stop. The most important element of the cessation process is the smoker's decision to quit, with the aid or method of secondary importance. However, those who use aids such as nicotine replacement therapy double

their chances of successfully quitting.[3] Smokers wishing to quit may find it helpful to telephone the national helpline on 0800 169 0169. Pregnant women seeking help in stopping smoking should call 0800 169 9169 where specialist counsellors are available from 1pm to 9pm, 7 days a week, to give advice. QUIT also operates specialist advice lines in the main Asian languages and in Turkish and Kurdish.

### Weight gain

The possibility of weight gain is often of particular concern to those who want to give up smoking. More than 80% of smokers will gain weight once they quit smoking, but the long-term weight gain is on average only 6-8lbs for each smoker who quits.[6] However, this is the weight gain made without recourse to any special attempts at dieting or exercise and it presents a minor health risk when compared to the risk of continued smoking. In addition, improved lung function and some of the other health benefits of giving up smoking are likely to make exercise both easier and more beneficial.

### Pipes and cigars

Some smokers switch to pipes or cigars in the belief that this is a less dangerous form of smoking. However, such smokers may incur the same risks and may even increase them, especially if they inhale the pipe or cigar smoke.[7]

### Smoking cessation aids

There are two proven pharmaceutical aids to stopping smoking: nicotine replacement therapy and bupropion, known by its tradename,

## Beneficial health changes when you stop smoking

Stop smoking and the body will begin to repair the damage done almost immediately, kick-starting a series of beneficial health changes that continue for years. [4]

| Time since quitting | Beneficial health changes that take place |
| --- | --- |
| 20 minutes | Blood pressure and pulse rate return to normal. |
| 8 hours | Nicotine and carbon monoxide levels in blood reduce by half, oxygen levels return to normal. |
| 24 hours | Carbon monoxide will be eliminated from the body. Lungs start to clear out mucus and other smoking debris. |
| 48 hours | There is no nicotine left in the body. Ability to taste and smell is greatly improved. |
| 72 hours | Breathing becomes easier. Bronchial tubes begin to relax and energy levels increase. |
| 2 – 12 weeks | Circulation improves. |
| 3 – 9 months | Coughs, wheezing and breathing problems improve as lung function is increased by up to 10%. |
| 1 year | Risk of a heart attack falls to about half that of a smoker. |
| 10 years | Risk of lung cancer falls to half that of a smoker. |
| 15 years | Risk of heart attack falls to the same as someone who has never smoked. |

Zyban. Nicotine replacement therapies (NRT), such as chewing gum, skin patch, tablet, nasal spray or inhaler, are designed to help the smoker to break the habit while providing a reduced dose of nicotine to overcome withdrawal symptoms such as craving and mood changes. Studies have shown that NRT roughly doubles the chances of a smoker successfully quitting compared to someone using no therapy.[8]

Bupropion (Zyban) works by de-sensitising the brain's nicotine receptors and has shown promising results in clinical trials. The course of treatment lasts around 8 weeks. It is only available on prescription under medical supervision. Zyban is safe for most healthy adults but there are side effects, the most serious of which is the risk of seizures (fits). This risk is estimated to be less than 1 in 1000 but other less serious side effects such as insomnia, dry mouth and headaches are more common. An independent review by the Consumers' Association concluded that 'when used in a specialist setting and in conjunction with regular counselling, bupropion is at least twice as effective as placebo in helping patients to stop smoking'.[9]

## Other cessation aids

### Acupuncture and hypnosis

A review of alternative methods of aids to stopping smoking found little evidence to support the effectiveness of either acupuncture or hypnosis as a means of stopping smoking, but such methods may suit some smokers.[10]

### Herbal cigarettes

These are not recommended as an aid to giving up smoking because they produce both tar and carbon monoxide. Some brands have a tar content equivalent to tobacco cigarettes. In addition, the use of herbal cigarettes reinforces the habit of smoking which smokers need to overcome.

### Clinics and self-help groups

Smokers who are motivated to quit the habit may benefit from cessation clinics or self-help groups, although smokers should be cautious about claims of high success rates made by some clinics. A review of smoking cessation products and services found that smokers are up to four times more likely to stop smoking by attending specialist smokers' clinics than by using willpower alone.[11] As part of the Government's review of the NHS, more smoking cessation clinics are being established by health authorities and primary care groups.[12]

### References

1 *Nicotine Addiction in Britain.* A report of the Royal College of Physicians, February 2000.

2 Lader, D and Meltzer, H. *Smoking related behaviour and attitudes, 1999.* Office for National Statistics, 2000.

3 Smoking cessation guidelines and their cost effectiveness. *Thorax* 1998; vol 53: S5 (part 2) S11-S16.

4 The Health Benefits of Smoking Cessation: A report of the Surgeon General. US DHHS, 1990.

5 West, R. *Tobacco withdrawal symptoms.* St. George's Hospital Medical School, 1996.

6 West, R. *Tobacco withdrawal symptoms.* St. George's Hospital Medical School, 1996.

7 *Cigars: Health effects and trends.* National Cancer Institute, 1998.

8 Nicotine replacement therapy for smoking cessation. *The Cochrane Library*, Issue 3, May 2001.

9 Bupropion to aid smoking cessation. *Drug and Therapeutics Bulletin.* Vol 38 no.10 Oct. 2000.

10 Abstracts of the Cochrane review. *The Cochrane Library*, Issue 3, 2001.

11 West, R. *Getting serious about stopping smoking – a review of products, services and techniques.* 1997.

12 Extract from the NHS National Plan – July 2000.

■ The above information is from Action on Smoking and Health – ASH. For further information visit their website which can be found at www.ash.org.uk

© Action on Smoking and Health – ASH

# Smoking ban 'would save 5,000 lives'

Nearly 5,000 lives would be saved per year if smoking was banned in public places – more than are lost annually in road accidents across Great Britain – anti-smoking campaigners claimed 10 March 2004.

No Smoking Day's campaign director, Ben Youdan, said banning tobacco in pubs, bars and all workplaces would save 4,800 lives a year in England, Wales and Scotland, almost 1,500 more than the 3,400 people killed on the roads each year.

Mr Youdan said outlawing smoking in the workplace would lead to half a million smokers giving up the habit and have four times more impact on current smoking levels than last year's tobacco advertising ban.

An estimated 1.25 million smokers attempt to beat their addiction on No Smoking Day and campaigners believe a change in the law would help them further.

Mr Youdan said: 'Eighty-five percent of former smokers actually support smoke-free public places because they fear that the tobacco temptation will be too great.

'We know from our research with smokers themselves that the pub is one of the times they're most at risk of relapsing.'

Further research published to coincide with No Smoking Day showed that almost a quarter (23%) of men's deaths and one in eight women's deaths, in London, was caused by smoking, accounting for 10,500 deaths in those aged over 35 each year.

The report by the campaign group SmokeFree London and the London Health Observatory also found that people with smoking-related diseases took up 1,100 of the capital's hospital beds every day. This is the equivalent of almost filling both Guy's and St Thomas's hospitals, costing the NHS at least £2m every week.

Dr Bobbie Jacobson, director of the observatory, said: 'That tobacco

causes preventable deaths is not new, but we were shocked by the scale of the burden of tobacco – both to Londoners and to the capital's health services.

'Our findings show that we must re-double our efforts to tackle the health divide caused by tobacco where the poorest smokers suffer most.'

Dr Konrad Jamrozik, professor of primary care epidemiology at London University's Imperial College, added: 'This report shows that tobacco is still the major cause of premature death in this city.

'While road traffic fatalities occur on London's busy streets at a rate of under one per day, one Londoner's life is stubbed out by smoking cigarettes every hour.'

Smoking is the biggest cause of preventable death in the UK, responsible for 120,000 premature deaths a year. It is estimated that there are more than 13 million smokers in Britain.

Dr Vivienne Nathanson, head of science and ethics at the British Medical Association, also renewed calls for a public smoking ban.

She said: 'Every day around three million employees are compelled to work in smoke-filled environments.

'This increases their risk of developing fatal illnesses like lung cancer or heart disease and damages the health of unborn children. Every year 1,200 low birth-weight babies are

born as a result of their mothers being exposed to second-hand smoke at work.

'We need a complete ban on smoking in the workplace. Partial restrictions are only partially effective, designated smoking areas do not work unless they are physically isolated from non-smoking areas and the evidence shows that conventional ventilation does not effectively protect non-smokers from the health effects of passive smoking.'

The British Thoracic Society (BTS) said every NHS hospital should have a stop smoking counsellor to help the hardcore of heavy smokers to quit.

*Family doctors in Gloucestershire are offering smokers a £20 reward if they quit for a month.*
The three GPs at the Frampton on Severn surgery are funding the initiative out of their own pockets to tie in with No Smoking Day.

One of the GPs, Charles Buckley, described the initiative as 'moral blackmail' and said he hoped it would provide an extra incentive to patients.

The practice has 4,500 patients on its books, around 20% of whom are smokers. The doctors believe up to 20 will succeed in the challenge.

■ This article first appeared in *The Guardian*, 10 March 2004.

# Government sets tougher smoking reduction target

*By Paul Stephenson*

The likely announcement of a much tougher government target for reducing the number of smokers in Britain has been welcomed by anti-smoking campaigners.

Although the government is already committed to reducing the proportion of smokers to 24% by 2010, the figure is likely to be revised to a lower figure of 21%, according to a leaked document seen by *Health Service Journal.*

The figure is included in a late draft copy of the Department of Health's targets for the Treasury's public service agreements, to cover the period 2005-2010. The draft confirmed that the DoH would reduce the proportion of adults smoking to significantly below half the level of 30 years ago, when 45% of adults smoked.

Since the government first published the target of 24% in 1998, progress has been ahead of initial plans, so the new target may well therefore be achievable.

The target of cutting the number of adult smokers to 26% by 2005 has already been achieved, as has the target of cutting smoking among 11- to 15-year-olds to 9% by 2010.

However, a figure of 21% would still be above the ideal figure discussed by Derek Wanless in his report on the future of funding for the health service.

In the scenario envisaged by Mr Wanless, in which the public is fully engaged in health improvement and progress on improving health is most rapid, the number of smokers would have to fall to 17% by 2011 and 11% by 2022.

> **The target of cutting the number of adult smokers to 26% by 2005 has already been achieved, as has the target of cutting smoking among 11- to 15-year-olds to 9% by 2010**

In a submission to the government last month, the public health charity Action on Smoking and Health (Ash) said: 'If current rates of decline in smoking prevalence continue, smoking prevalence will still be at 22% by 2011, and it would take 20 years to reach Californian levels of 17%.'

However, the director of Ash, Deborah Arnott, told SocietyGuardian.co.uk that the 21% target was a significant move. She said: 'Instead of being internal Department of Health targets, they are going to be public service agreement targets. [These] are much more significant.'

But Ms Arnott said that the government should be aiming for 17%. 'I think 21% is still not enough, but it is a step in the right direction and, more importantly, it being a public service agreement target is a very important development.'

Ms Arnott said several factors would help people to quit smoking. She said the full effect of the ban on tobacco advertising had yet to come through and any future legislation on smoke-free workplaces would have a significant impact on reducing smoking.

The Department of Health refused to comment on the leaked draft, but said the targets had not yet been finalised.

■ This article first appeared in *The Guardian*, 11 June 2004.

© Paul Stephenson

■ There are about 12 million adult cigarette smokers in Great Britain and another 1.3 million who smoke pipes and/or cigars. (p. 1)

■ Smoking prevalence is highest in the 20-24 age group for both men and women but thereafter in older age groups there are progressively fewer smokers. (p. 1)

■ Around one in ten teenagers in the UK is a regular smoker. By age 15, more than one in five smokes regularly. (p. 2)

■ Mounting evidence over the last two decades has shown that exposure to secondhand smoke, or passive smoking is harmful to adult and child health. (p. 3)

■ Of all the stuff crammed into a smoke, the three biggest harmful components are nicotine, carbon monoxide and tar. (p. 4)

■ The damage to health may be caused by the tar and poisonous chemicals, but it's the nicotine in tobacco which smokers can grow to depend upon. (p. 4)

■ For most of the twentieth century, men smoked considerably more heavily than women. The gap has narrowed fast in recent decades. Now 28% of UK men, and 26% of UK women, smoke. Teenage girls, though, smoke more, a lot more, than teenage boys: 26%:21% at 15. (p. 5)

■ While, and until, adult smoking is tackled, teenagers will smoke and will do themselves irreparable harm. (p. 6)

■ By the age of 15 years around one in four children in England are regular smokers, despite the fact that it is illegal to sell any tobacco product to people under 16. Since the mid 1980s girls have been more likely to smoke regularly than boys. (p. 8)

■ Children are far more likely to smoke if other people at home smoke. It appears that a sibling smoking has even more influence than a parent smoking. (p. 8)

■ One in two smokers will die prematurely; 40% of heavy smokers die before retirement age, compared to 15% of non-smokers. (p. 9)

■ Smoking causes approximately 82% of all deaths from lung cancer, 83% of all deaths from bronchitis and emphysema and about 25% of all deaths from heart disease. (p. 10)

■ With one major exception (lung cancer), none of the illnesses described as 'smoking-related' is exclusive to smokers and all are primarily diseases of the elderly. In reality, two-thirds of all deaths in the UK are caused by 'smoking-related diseases', despite the fact that only half of those people actually smoke. (p. 11)

■ The debate on environmental tobacco smoke is far from over, contrary to what many people say. (p. 12)

■ There will be 1,000 million (1 billion) tobacco deaths world-wide in the 21st century if current global smoking patterns continue – a tenfold increase on the 20th-century toll of 100 million. (p. 14)

■ The UK and the USA have among the highest rates of lung cancer in women in the world at present. However, both countries have the fastest falling rates of lung cancer in men. (p. 15)

■ Around 38,000 cases of lung cancer are diagnosed annually – 90 per cent of them caused by cigarettes – and only 5 per cent of victims live for more than five years. (p. 16)

■ A killer on the loose reveals that in the UK around 900 office workers, 165 bar workers and 145 manufacturing workers die each year as a direct result of breathing in other people's tobacco smoke at work. (p. 17)

■ Britain's most senior doctors called yesterday for a ban on smoking in public places. They estimate that it could save 160,000 lives. (p. 19)

■ 'Smoking isn't a crime and it is important that politicians recognise that smokers need somewhere where they can smoke in comfort without being ostracised from their non-smoking friends, the majority of whom want restrictions, not a total ban.' (p. 21)

■ The Tobacco Advertising and Promotion Act came into effect on 14 February 2003. The Act outlaws adverts for cigarettes in magazines, newspapers, on the internet and on billboards. Sponsorship of Formula 1 racing and other 'global sporting events' will continue until 2006 at the latest. (p. 26)

■ Set a date – commit yourself to a stop date well in advance. Women should choose a date during the two weeks after the start of their period to experience less withdrawal symptoms. (p. 35)

■ Surveys have consistently shown that at least 70% of adult smokers would like to stop smoking. (p. 36)

■ The target of cutting the number of adult smokers to 26% by 2005 has already been achieved, as has the target of cutting smoking among 11- to 15-year-olds to 9% by 2010. (p. 39)

# ADDITIONAL RESOURCES

You might like to contact the following organisations for further information. Due to the increasing cost of postage, many organisations cannot respond to enquiries unless they receive a stamped, addressed envelope.

*ASH – Action on Smoking and Health*
102 Clifton Street
London, EC2A 4HW
Tel: 020 7739 5902
Fax: 020 7613 0531
E-mail: enquiries@ash.org.uk
Website: www.ash.org.uk
Tobacco is unique: the only product that kills when used normally – 120,000 deaths per year in the UK. ASH is leading the fight to control the tobacco epidemic and to confront the lies and dirty tricks of the tobacco industry.

*British Heart Foundation (BHF)*
14 Fitzhardinge Street
London, W1H 4DH
Tel: 020 7935 0185
Fax: 020 7486 5820
Website: www.bhf.org.uk
The aim of the British Heart Foundation is to play a leading role in the fight against heart disease and prevent death by ways including educating the public and health professionals about heart disease, its prevention and treatment.

*Cancer Research UK*
PO Box 123
Lincoln's Inn Fields
London, WC2A 3PX
Tel: 020 7242 0200
Fax: 020 7269 3262
E-mail: publications@cancer.org.uk
Website: www.cancerresearchuk.org
www.lowtarexposed.org
The vision of Cancer Research UK is to conquer cancer through world-class research.

*The Coronary Prevention Group*
2 Taviton Street
London, WC1H 0BT
Tel: 020 7927 2125
Fax: 020 7927 2127
E-mail: cpg@lshtm.ac.uk
Website: www.healthnet.org.uk
Contributes to the prevention of coronary heart disease, the UK's major cause of death. Provides information to the public on all preventable risk factors – smoking, high blood pressure and raised blood cholesterol – and advice on healthy eating, exercise and stress.

*FOREST (Freedom Organisation for the Right to Enjoy Smoking)*
Audley House
13 Palace Street
London, SW1E 5HX
Tel: 07071 766537
Fax: 020 7630 6226
E-mail: choice@forestonline.org
Website: www.forestonline.org
Defends adult freedom of choice against prohibitionists, social authoritarians and medical paternalists. FOREST does not promote smoking. Campaigns through publishing, organising conferences and demonstrations. FOREST will provide further information upon receipt of a formal request from teachers but will not supply information to any person under the age of 18 years.

*No Smoking Day*
59 Redchurch Street
London, E2 7DJ
Tel: 0870 7707909
Fax: 0870 7707910
E-mail: enquiries@nosmokingday.org.uk
Website: www.nosmokingday.org.uk
A national campaign organised by a committee of 14 agencies representing a collaboration of public, professional and voluntary partners, all with an interest in reducing smoking-related disease. Produces an annual campaign pack which includes leaflets, posters, factsheets and runs the Quitline 0800 00 22 00.

*QUIT*
Victory House
170 Tottenham Court Road
London, W1P 0HA
Tel: 020 7251 1551
Fax: 020 7251 1661
E-mail: quit-projects@clara.co.uk
Website: www.quit.org.uk
Works to provide practical help, advice and support to all smokers who want to stop. Ring the Freephone Quitline on 0800 00 22 00.

*The Roy Castle Lung Cancer Foundation*
International Centre for Lung Cancer Research
200 London Road
Liverpool, L3 9TA
Tel: 0871 2205426
Fax: 0151 794 8888
E-mail: foundation@roycastle.org
Website: www.roycastle.org/kats/
The Roy Castle International Centre for Lung Cancer Research is a UK charity and research centre, dedicated to defeating lung cancer. Runs the Kids Against Tobacco Smoke education service.

*Tobacco Manufacturers' Association (TMA)*
5th Floor, Burwood House
14/16 Caxton Street
London, SW1H 0ZB
Tel: 020 7544 0100
Fax: 020 7544 0117
E-mail: information@the-tma.org.uk
Website: www.the-tma.org.uk
The Tobacco Manufacturers' Association (TMA) is the trade association for those companies which manufacture tobacco products in the UK. Its prime function is to represent the UK tobacco manufacturers.

*YouthNet UK*
2-3 Upper Street
Islington
London, N1 0PH
Tel: 020 7226 8008
Fax: 020 7226 8118
E-mail: info@thesite.org
Web-site: www.thesite.org
TheSite.org is produced and managed by YouthNet UK. TheSite.org aims to offer the best guide to life for young adults, aged 16-25.

# INDEX

# ACKNOWLEDGEMENTS

The publisher is grateful for permission to reproduce the following material.

While every care has been taken to trace and acknowledge copyright, the publisher tenders its apology for any accidental infringement or where copyright has proved untraceable. The publisher would be pleased to come to a suitable arrangement in any such case with the rightful owner.

### Chapter One: The Smoking Debate

*Who smokes and how much?*, © Action on Smoking and Health – ASH, *Smoking statistics*, © British Heart Foundation, *Smoking and age*, © ASH/Crown copyright is reproduced with the permission of Her Majesty's Stationery Office, *Anatomy of a cigarette*, © www.thesite.org, *Real drag*, © QUIT, *Regular smokers*, © National Centre for Social Research and the National Foundation for Educational Research, *Chocolate in tobacco 'to attract children'*, © Telegraph Group Limited, London 2004, *Children and smoking*, © Cancer Research UK, *Smoking and your health*, © Coronary Prevention Group, *What smoking does to your body*, © Crown copyright is reproduced with the permission of Her Majesty's Stationery Office, *Smoking and disease*, © KATS (Kids against tobacco smoke) – The Roy Castle Lung Cancer Foundation, *Smoking and health*, © FOREST, *Passive smoking may not damage your health*, © Telegraph Group Limited, London 2004, *Double the danger for passive smokers*, © 2004 Associated New Media, *Smoking and cancer*, © Cancer Research UK, *Lung cancer*, © Cancer Research UK, *Smokers at cancer risk even after cutting back*, © The Daily Mail, January 2004, *Smoke screen*, © Hazards Publications Ltd, *Strong support for workplace smoking law*, © MORI, *Ban smoking in public, say top doctors*, © Telegraph Group Limited, London 2004, *What people really think about public smoking*, © Tobacco Manufacturers' Association, *Fight for choice*, © FOREST, *Smoking in public places*, © FOREST, *Is this the end of smoking in public?*, © 2004 Associated New Media.

### Chapter Two: Quitting Smoking

*Want out of smoking?*, © No Smoking Day, *Smoking*, © National Youth Agency (NYA), *The QUIT guide to teen quitting*, © QUIT, *Stopping smoking*, © Action on Smoking and Health – ASH, *How smoking habit will cut 10 years off your life*, © The Daily Mail, June 2004, *Never smoked*, © Crown copyright is reproduced with the permission of Her Majesty's Stationery Office, *Low tar exposed*, © Cancer Research UK, *Thinking about giving up?*, © Crown copyright is reproduced with the permission of Her Majesty's Stationery Office, *In the clear*, © SCAPE, *What happens when you stop smoking*, © Action on Smoking and Health – ASH, *Smoking ban 'would save 5,000 lives'*, © Press Association, *Government sets tougher smoking reduction target*, © Paul Stephenson.

### Photographs and illustrations:

Pages 1, 25, 36: Don Hatcher; pages 4, 16, 30, 39: Simon Kneebone; pages 8, 23: Pumpkin House; pages 11, 29, 38: Angelo Madrid; pages 12, 26: Bev Aisbett.

Craig Donnellan
Cambridge
September, 2004